NOSTALGIA PATCHWORK & QUILTING

by Robby Savonen
Photographs by Jon Aron

Meredith® Press
New York, NY

Acknowledgments

I would like to thank the following craftspersons for their generous contributions to this book: Donna Bailey-Gates, Carol Lindquist, Patricia Loiacono, Kate McCombe, Nancy Moore.

Special thanks to Donna Bailey-Gates for allowing us to photograph in her lovely 1800s house on Nantucket Island; Sheila Yates for introducing us to her mother, Patricia Loiacono; Concord Fabrics for their contributions; and the Fairfield Processing Corporation for providing Poly-Fil.

Meredith® Press is an imprint of Meredith® Books:
President, Book Group: Joseph J. Ward
Vice President, Editorial Director: Elizabeth P. Rice

For Meredith Press:
Executive Editor: Maryanne Bannon
Senior Editor: Carol Spier
Associate Editors: Guido Anderau, Carolyn Mitchell
Copy Editor: Susanna Pfeffer
Production Manager: Bill Rose
Book Design: Remo Cosentino
Photography/Illustrations: Jon Aron

ISBN: 0-696-02468-3 (Hardcover)
ISBN: 0-696-20239-4 (Softcover)
Library of Congress Catalog Card Number: 93-077500

Printed in the United States of America
10 9 8 7 6 5 4 3 2 1

✦ CONTENTS ✦

INDEX   144

Dear Quilter:

Thank you for selecting *Nostalgia Patchwork & Quilting*, the seventh in a series of quilting annuals from Meredith® Press. We are delighted to present this wonderful collection of quilt projects that are both nostalgic and new.

Though the quilts shown are vintage 20s and 30s, the designs are timeless. Beautiful and practical in their era, they may surprise you with their longevity. We hope you'll enjoy recreating these quilts; many of the fabrics typical of this period are again available, and await your modern interpretations.

We at Meredith® Press strive to bring you high-quality craft books filled with projects you'll want to embark on for years to come. We include accurate instructions, full-size patterns, and myriad end uses in every book we create. Interesting motifs and vibrant color photos are featured throughout.

The publishers and the family of quilters and designers involved in the making of *Nostalgia Patchwork & Quilting* look fondly on the light colors and whimsical fabrics favored by quilters during the Depression. May the character and history conveyed by these quilts inspire your own needlework, which will no doubt be cherished long into the future.

Sincerely,

Carol Spier
Senior Editor

✦ INTRODUCTION ✦

While most of us know that quiltmaking is enormously successful today, it is fascinating to find out facts and trivia about quiltmaking in the not-so-distant past. I became interested in quilts of the 1920s and 30s, my grandmother's era, when the editors at Meredith Press and the Better Homes and Gardens Book Clubs discovered a number of quilts from that period. The patterns were familiar, since our studio had been working with early American quilts for years, but they were somehow different as well. The fabric colors and prints were vibrant and lively, and of course most of them were elaborately quilted. In those days women had more time, and often several women worked on one quilt over a period of months.

When looking at these vintage quilts it's interesting to think about what was happening in the country and how quilting fit into the lifestyle of the times. During the Depression quilting was an ideal escape from everyday worries as well as being a thrifty outlet for creativity.

In the 1920s women's magazines promoted quiltmaking by offering patterns and directions as well as mail-order kits. In the midwestern states, many local newspapers ran regular quilting columns that were enormously successful and increased readership among women. Quilting also proved to be the ideal way to increase the sale of fabrics, previously purchased for making clothing and curtains. Department stores began to feature quilt demonstrations to encourage sales.

By the 1930s and 40s the manufacturing of cotton fabrics had greatly improved. A dazzling array of colors was offered, and prints abounded, with large florals and allover patterns. These contributed to the excitement of quiltmaking, going beyond the necessity of making something utilitarian.

Most of the projects in this book are actual old quilts or have been made from parts of old quilts or textiles. For example, the quilt on page 34, called "World Without End," was one found by Kate McCombe, who often contributes to our books. She graciously allowed us to borrow it because the fabrics and pattern so perfectly represent the period in which it was made. The instructions enable you to reproduce the projects from new or old fabrics, using easy, contemporary methods.

My advice to you when making the projects that follow is to have fun finding fabric. This is the key to a project with a 1920s or 30s spirit. If your mother or grandmother is a fabric saver, go through her basket of scraps to look for material that might work for you. Perhaps years from now quilters will be adapting our original designs, making them better and improving on our technique in ways we can't begin to imagine.

I hope you'll enjoy recreating something from this period for future generations in your family. It will always evoke nostalgic feelings.

✦ QUILTING TERMS ✦

Before starting any quilting project it's a good idea to learn the basic terms of the craft. Quilting has been popular for such a long time that many different teachers have developed their own particular way of doing things. Often a quilter who has had success with a pattern will be excited enough to repeat it with different fabrics. This is how shortcuts and new ways to do the same things over and over are devised and often passed along from one quilter to another.

Familiarize yourself with the basic terms before you begin so the directions for each project will be clearer. Knowing what's involved before you begin will help you decide which project you'd like to make. You can refer to the basic terms from time to time if needed.

Backing: This is the fabric that backs the quilt. (See **Fabric** for types of material to use.) I've given the exact measurement needed for the backing of each project, but if you have extra backing fabric around the quilt top you should trim it *after* all quilting is complete, not before.

Basting: Long, loose stitches used to hold the top, batting, and backing together before quilting. These stitches are removed after each section is quilted.

Batting: The soft inner layer that gives the quilt dimension and warmth. Batting comes in various thicknesses, each appropriate for a different kind of project. Most quilts are made with a thin layer of batting, which may be made of polyester, cotton, or a blend. Quilt batting is sold by the yard and in sizes to fit different bed sizes. For this reason I've used the exact size of the quilt to give the measurement of the batting needed for each project. In this way you can buy the package of batting closest to the size needed. However, when quilting it's always a good idea to use batting several inches larger than the quilt top you are making. You can always trim the excess later.

For stuffing projects such as sachets, pin cushions, and pillows, you can buy packages of polyester fiberfill.

Binding: The way the raw edges of fabric are finished. Many quiltmakers cut the backing slightly larger than the quilt top all around so they can bring the extra fabric forward to finish the edges. Contrasting fabric or bias binding can also be used.

Block: Geometric or symmetrical pieces of fabric sewn together to create a design. The finished blocks are sewn together to create the finished quilt top. Individual blocks are often large enough to be used for a matching pillow. If you're a beginning quilter you might enjoy making a pillow as a first project.

Borders: Fabric strips that frame the pieced design. A border can be narrow or wide, and sometimes there is more than one border around a quilt. Borders that frame quilt blocks are called sashing. Borders may be made from one of the fabrics used in the design or from a contrasting fabric. Borders are often used to enlarge a quilt top so that it extends over the edges of the bed.

Traditionally, for the sake of interest, quilting patterns are stitched in the borders. However, many quilters leave this area free of stitches in order to complete the project in a shorter period of time. Borders are usually the largest pieces of fabric to be cut and should be cut in continuous strips, without piecing, for a nicer-looking quilt or wallhanging. Before you cut the smaller patches, mark off the border strips, allowing a few extra inches of length, but do not cut them until your quilt top is pieced, then check the length of each edge.

Patchwork: Fabric pieces sewn together to create a design, often a geometric block. The blocks are then sewn together to make the quilt top.

Piecing: Joining patchwork pieces together to form a design or a block.

Quilting: Stitching together two layers of fabric with a layer of batting between them.

Quilting patterns: The lines or markings on the fabric that make up the design. Small hand or machine stitches are made along these lines, which may be straight, curved, or made up of elaborate curlicue patterns. Small quilting stitches can also follow the seamlines where pieces of fabric are joined. Or, a quilting pattern can be created by stitching a grid or diamonds over the entire fabric.

Sashing: The narrow pieces of fabric used to frame the individual blocks and join them together (also known as lattice strips). They are often made in a contrasting color.

Setting: Joining the quilt blocks in rows to form the finished top of the quilt. Rows may be joined horizontally, vertically, or diagonally.

Top: The top of a quilting project is the decorative upper layer of fabric with the design showing. Patchwork or appliquéd pieces create the top.

Materials for Quilting

Cutting mat: This is a handy item for the quick measuring and cutting methods you'll use for making quilts. It is intended for use with a rotary cutter, and is available in fabric stores or from mail-order sources.

Fabric: You can never have too many different fabric patterns when designing a quilting project. I always seem to need 10 times more variety to choose from than I think. Fabric is the main concern: what kind, how much, and what colors or prints will work together.

Most quilters prefer 100% cotton, and most fabrics are 45 inches wide with selvage. All the fabrics you choose for a quilting project should be of the same weight and should be washed before using. This removes any sizing in the fabric and allows for shrinkage before making the project. Sometimes cotton fabric fades slightly. This produces a worn, old look which is desirable in the world of quiltmaking.

When collecting a variety of fabric prints for your quilting projects, it's a good idea to have a selection of lights and darks. The colors and patterns of the fabric will greatly affect the design. Calico has always been used for quilting projects. The small, allover prints can be used effectively together, and there is a wide variety of colors to choose from. Pretty floral prints are lovely to use with alternating solid colors chosen to match the colors in the prints.

The backing fabric for a quilt can be a sheet, muslin, or one of the fabrics used for the patchwork on the top. It too should be 100% cotton. A light color is generally thought to be better than a dark color, which might show through the thin batting and light fabric in the quilt top. Unlike 45-inch wide fabric, a sheet of the appropriate size should be wide enough to cover the back of any size quilt without piecing.

Iron: It's impossible to work on any project without having an iron right next to the sewing machine. After each stitching step, you will be instructed to press the fabric. If you are doing patchwork, it's handy to pad a stool or chair with a piece of batting and place it next to you by the sewing machine. As you piece the fabric, you can press the seams (see **Seam allowances**) without getting up. Use a steam setting.

Marking pen: Sometimes a pattern or design has to be traced and transferred to the fabric. When you want an allover quilting design, you'll need lines to follow. Water-soluble marking pens made specifically for marking your quilting lines on the fabric can be found in fabric shops. Once you've finished quilting, the pen marks can be removed with a plant mister or damp sponge. Simply pat over the lines and they'll disappear.

Colored chalk pencils are used for marking quilting patterns on dark fabric. They come in all colors including white, and when the quilting is complete the chalk is easily brushed away.

Needles: All the projects in this book are pieced on a sewing machine. The quilting can be done by hand or machine, but hand quilting looks best. If the batting is very thick, it will not go through the machine and the quilting must be done by hand. Many quilters use this thick batting for tied quilts. However, most quilts are made with traditional thin batting. To quilt you'll need #7 and #8 "betweens," the most common size of needles used for hand quilting, or "sharps," which are longer and have a slightly larger eye.

Rotary cutter: This tool looks like a pizza cutter and allows you to cut several layers of fabric at once. It is more accurate than scissors.

Ruler and yardstick: You can't work without them. A metal ruler can be used as a straightedge for the most accurate cutting. Use the yardstick for cutting lengths of fabric where you must mark and cut at least 36 inches at one time.

Stitch Diagrams

Running Stitch

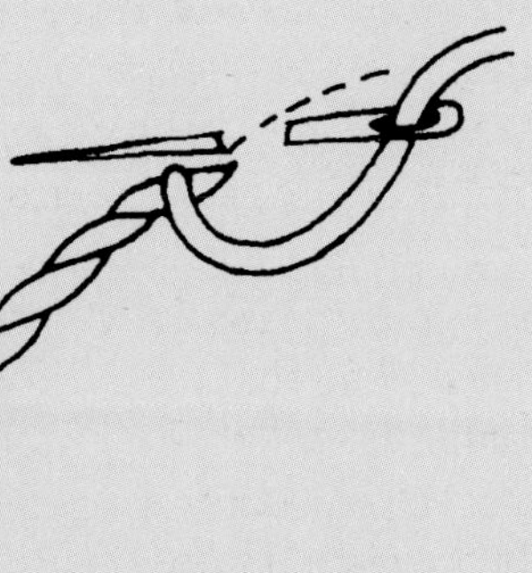

Stem/Outline Stitch

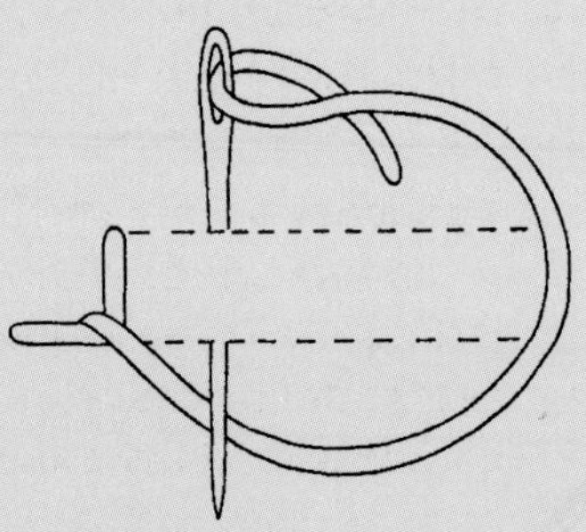

Blanket Stitch — Step 1

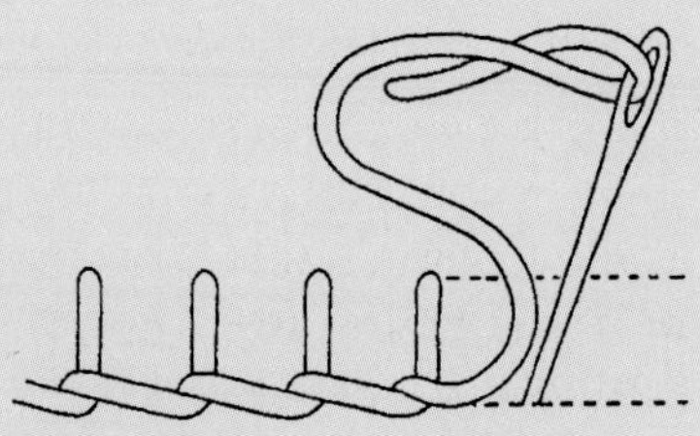

Blanket Stitch — Step 2

Slipstitch

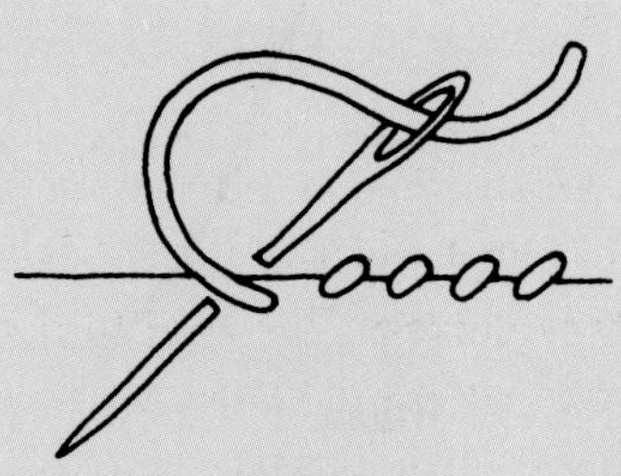

Overcast Stitch

The width of the yardstick is perfect for marking a grid pattern for quilting. You simply draw the first line, then flip the yardstick over and continue to mark lines without ever removing the yardstick from the fabric. You will have a perfect 1-inch grid (see **Allover quilting**).

Scissors: You'll need good scissors for cutting your fabric. Try not to use these scissors to cut anything but fabric to keep them at their best. Cutting paper with scissors can dull them. Invest in a pair of small, pointed scissors for snipping threads as you stitch and quilt.

Stencil: Many quilt patterns are available on precut stencil paper. This makes it easier to plan and transfer the designs to the fabric. You position the stencil on the fabric and mark through the cut lines onto the fabric. Some quilters like making their own stencils. Materials are available in art supply and hobby shops.

Straight pins: Use extra long 1¾-inch sharp pins.

Template: A rigid, full-size pattern that is used to trace design elements. It can be cut from cardboard, manila, oaktag (used for file folders), plastic, acetate, or sandpaper. Acetate, which is transparent and produces clean, crisp edges, is ideal for pattern pieces when a repeat design is required. Sandpaper doesn't slip when placed face down on the fabric. If you're cutting a single design, simply use the paper pattern pinned to the fabric as a cutting guide. Templates for patchwork pieces usually include seam allowance; those for appliqués often do not. Some quilters prefer to use templates without seam allowances, adding their own as they cut.

Thimble: I can't work with one, but I try to from time to time because my fingers are numb from pricking them so often. Try a thimble for hand quilting, but be sure to get the right size. I must admit, without it I run the risk of bleeding on my fabric.

Thread: Match the thread to the color of the fabric. Cotton-blend thread is best for all quilting and piecing.

Techniques

Estimating fabric yardage: The fabric used for all of these projects is 45 inches wide. All measurements include ¼-inch seam allowance unless otherwise specified.

Every project lists the exact amount of fabric needed for each color, and all the quilt projects are made to fit standard bed sizes. However, if you want to be sure that a specific quilt will fit your special needs, or if you want to change the size specified to something larger or smaller, it's easy to figure what size will best fit your bed.

When estimating yardage for a bed quilt, measure your bed fully made up. This means with bed pad, sheets and blankets over the mattress. Measure the length, width and depth, including the box spring.

Decide if you want a slight overhang, an overhang to the top of a dust ruffle, or a drop to the floor (if so, measure the distance from the top of the mattress to the floor), and whether you want the quilt to extend up and over the pillows. If a quilt isn't the right size for your bed, it can be changed by adding to, or subtracting from, the border measurements. This shouldn't change the basic design.

Piecing the backing: You may have to piece panels together for the backing of a quilt, tablecloth, or wallhanging in order to get the correct size. Use the full width of fabric (usually 45 inches), cut to the appropriate length. Cut another length the same size. Then cut this length in half lengthwise so that you have two narrow strips of the same size. Join one of these strips to the corresponding edges of the large center panel to avoid a seam down the middle of the backing. Press the seams open. Trim backing to the size given in the instructions. If you use a bed sheet the same size as the quilt top you will have a backing that doesn't require piecing (see **Fabric**).

Transferring a design: Trace the pattern pieces or quilting design. Place a piece of dressmaker's carbon on the right side of the fabric with the carbon side down and trace design over it. Go over all pattern lines with a tracing wheel or ballpoint pen to transfer the design. Remove the carbon and tracing.

Preparing appliqués: An appliqué is a fabric shape applied to another fabric. The edges of the appliqué fabric shape are usually turned under and hand-stitched to the background fabric. Appliqués may also be applied with machine zigzag stitching.

Making a template: Templates may be made from heavy paper such as oaktag, manila, thin cardboard, or sandpaper, or from clear acetate. If you use heavy paper you'll have to transfer the pattern to the template material. First trace the design, using pencil and tracing paper. Then place the tracing face down on the template material and, using a pen or pencil, rub over each traced line to transfer the design. Remove the tracing and go over the lines with a ballpoint pen to make them more visible. You can also use carbon paper to transfer the design. Cut out the design outline from the template material.

There are several advantages to using acetate for your template material. Since it's clear, you can trace a pattern piece directly onto it. It can be used many times without losing its sharp edges. Further, you can see through it when placing it on your fabric in order to position it where you want it. In this way, if you are using a floral print, for example, you can center a flower in the middle of the template piece.

Determine which template(s) will be used for each fabric. If seam allowances are not already included, place the templates at least ½ inch apart to allow for the ¼-inch seam allowance when cutting out each piece.

Consider the grain of the fabric and the direction of the print when placing your templates.

Freezer paper templates: This is a quick-and-easy method for cutting appliqués. It is especially good for cutting small or narrow pieces such as stems for flowers. Freezer paper, which is sold in the wrap section of supermarkets, is polyethylene-coated. (Do not use waxed paper.) One side of the paper is shiny, the other dull. It is translucent so you can place it over the pattern piece and trace it. With the dull side up, trace the shape, then cut it out and place it shiny side down on the wrong side of your appliqué fabric. Press the paper with a hot iron; the paper will adhere to the fabric temporarily. Then, cut around the shape, adding ¼-inch seam allowance all around on the fabric. Clip into the seam allowance at evenly spaced intervals, then press the fabric over the edge of the freezer paper template. Peel away the freezer paper, turn the appliqué over and press again to make sharp edges and nicely rounded curves. The freezer paper template can be reused three or four times before losing its adhesiveness.

Sewing points: Many traditional quilt patterns are created from triangles, diamonds, and similar shapes. The points present a challenge and require special care.

When stitching two such pieces together, first mark the finished points with a pin. Then, beginning and ending your seams at these marks, sew along the seamline, but do not sew into the seam allowance at each point.

Seam allowances: After stitching each seam and before crossing with another seam, press the seam allowances as directed. Note that the expression "press seams to one side" means to press the seam allowances to one side.

Sewing curves: Before turning under the edges of a curved appliqué piece, staystitch along the seamline, then clip or notch evenly spaced cuts into the seam allowance up to the staystitching. Clip all inward curves and notch all outward curves. When the fabric is turned under and pressed, it will lie flat.

Sewing inside corner edges: Staystitch the corner along the seamline. Place a pin across the point of the stitches and clip into the seam allowance up to the stitches in order to turn the fabric under.

Outside corner edge: Once you've stitched around a corner, clip off half the seam allowance across the point. Turn fabric back, press seams open, and trim excess fabric away.

Turning corners: It's often a bit difficult to turn corners and continue a seam line. Figure 1 shows the 3 pieces to be joined. With right sides together, stitch piece A to piece B as shown in Figure 2. Next, join C to A, as shown in Figure 3. Leave the needle down in the fabric. Lift the

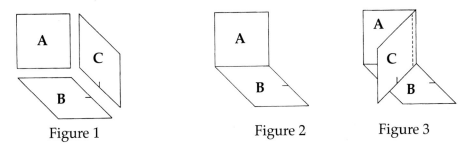

Figure 1	Figure 2	Figure 3

presser foot and clip the seam allowance to the needle. Slide B under C and adjust so the edges of B align with C. Lower the presser foot and stitch along the seamline.

Quilting

Quilting is sewing layers of fabric and batting together with small, even, straight running stitches in a decorative pattern. The quilting process, generally the finishing step in a patchwork or appliqué project, is what makes the project interesting and gives it a padded, textured look.

Allover quilting: When you want to fill large areas of the background with quilting, choose a simple design. The background quilting should not interfere with the patchwork or appliqué elements.

To ensure accurate spacing, make grid patterns of squares or diamond shapes with a yardstick or masking tape. For a quick-and-easy method, lay a yardstick diagonally across the fabric and mark it with a marking pen. Without removing the yardstick turn it over and mark along the edge once again. Continue across the fabric to the opposite edge. You will have perfect 1-inch spaces between the lines. Lay the yardstick across the fabric at the corner adjacent to where you began and repeat the process to create a 1-inch grid. Quilt along these lines.

Basting: Before quilting, you will have to baste the quilt top, batting and backing together. To avoid a lump of filler at any point, begin at the center of the top and baste outward with long, loose stitches, to create a sunburst pattern. There should be about 6 inches between the basted lines at the edges of the quilt. Baste from the top side only. These stitches will be cut away as you do your quilting.

Hand quilting: Thread your needle with a length of approximately 18 to 20 inches and make a small knot with a 1-inch tail beyond it. Bring the needle up through the backing to the quilt top where the first line of quilting will begin and give the knotted end a good tug to pull it through the backing into the batting. Take small running stitches. Follow your premarked quilting pattern or stitch ¼ inch away from each side of all seamlines. Do not stitch into the ¼-inch seam allowance around the outside edge of the quilt.

Machine quilting: This quicker way to create a quilted look does not create the same rich look of authentic, early quilting that hand stitching does. It is best to machine-quilt when the batting isn't too thick.

When machine quilting, set the stitch length at approximately 6 stitches to the inch so the stitching looks more like hand stitching. Taking this precaution will ensure that the absence of hand stitching doesn't detract from the design. You may need to loosen the tension, too.

Outlining: This is a method of quilting along the patchwork seams. In this way, each design element is accented and the fabric layers are secured.

Tie quilting: An alternative to hand quilting is tying at evenly spaced intervals to hold the backing, batting and quilt top together. This is usually done with embroidery floss in the center of blocks and at the corners where blocks intersect as follows: Thread the needle with a length of floss approximately 10 to 12 inches, but do not knot the end. Insert the needle through the top of the quilt through all 3 layers and bring it back up again close to where you first inserted the needle. Tie the floss in a double knot and cut the ends to approximately 1½ inches.

Quick-and-Easy Methods

Strip piecing: This is a method by which you sew strips of different fabrics together and cut them into units that are arranged to make up the entire quilt top. This method is especially helpful when the project requires the piecing together of small or narrow pieces of fabric of the same size. Rather than cutting and sewing individual squares together over and over again, two or more strips of fabric are sewn together and then cut into segments of identical dimensions. These units are then arranged and stitched together in different positions to form the quilt pattern.

Right triangles: There is a quick-and-easy way to make perfect pieced triangles to create squares of any size. You can mark and stitch right-angle triangles before cutting. This is usually done when you want to create a square made up of one light and one dark triangle.

1. Begin by determining the number of pieced squares you'll need for the project. In the next step, you'll create a grid of squares on the wrong side of a piece of fabric, usually the lighter color. The number of squares will be *half* the number of squares needed for the project, because you'll get *two* triangle pairs from each square on the grid.

2. Determine the size of your finished square and add ⅞ inch to it. For example, if you want to create 2-inch squares, mark off a grid of 2⅞-inch squares on the wrong side of the light fabric. It's a good idea to draw a few extra squares in case you make an error in stitching.

3. Next, draw diagonal lines through each square as shown in Figure 1. With right sides together and raw edges aligned, pin the marked light

Strip Piecing

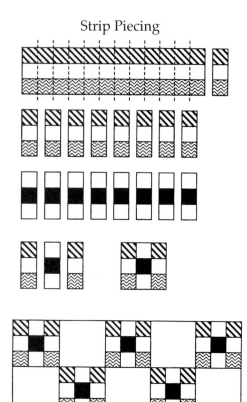

fabric to the same size dark fabric. Stitch ¼ inch away from each side of the drawn diagonal lines as shown in Figure 2.

4. Cut on all grid (diagonal, vertical and horizontal) lines to get the individual squares of contrasting fabric triangles. You'll have two triangles in each square (see Figure 3). Press seams to the dark side.

Binding a quilt: One way to finish a quilt is to hold the edges in place with a narrow binding all around. Some quilters like to use the backing to bind the edges and often choose one of the fabrics from the pieced top for this purpose. To use the backing to create a binding and narrow border all around the quilt you will need to cut the backing at least 1 inch larger than the finished top all around. Once the quilting is complete, turn the raw edges of the backing forward ¼ inch and press. Then, folding the corners neatly, turn this fabric forward to cover the raw edges of the quilt top and press. Pin in place and hand- or machine-stitch all around.

Purchased binding is made from bias strips of fabric sewn together. You will find packages of bias binding in a variety of colors in most fabric shops. Several seams will be visible at intervals along the binding, but this is acceptable. It's not always easy to match the color exactly to those in your fabrics. Some quilters make their own bias binding by cutting bias strips of fabric to match one of the fabrics in the quilt top and stitching them together to create the length of binding needed.

Hanging a quilt: Only quilts that are in good condition and not too heavy should be hung. There are three reliable methods for hanging a quilt or wall hanging. I prefer using a Velcro® strip, which is effective if the quilt or wall hanging is lightweight and not too large. For this method, machine-stitch the non-gripping side of the Velcro® to a strip of cotton tape, which is then hand-sewn to the back top edge of the quilt. Sew the tape to the backing fabric and batting only, not through to the quilt top, and stop short of each end. The gripping side of the Velcro® is then glued to a length of lath (available in lumber yards) slightly shorter than the width of the quilt. Nail the lath to the wall and then attach the quilt to the lath. You may want to treat the bottom of the quilt in the same way.

For heavier quilts the following method is preferable: Make a fabric sleeve approximately 3½ to 4 inches deep and an inch shorter at each end than the width of the quilt. Hand-sew it to the back of the top edge of the quilt, sewing through the backing and batting only. Insert a thin piece of wood, curtain rod, or dowel through the sleeve and suspend it at each end on brackets or other hangers.

An alternative for a light quilt or wall hanging is to use Velcro® to attach it to a set of artist's stretcher bars. These are available in various sizes in art supply stores.

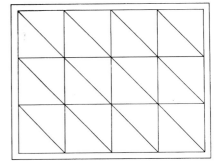

Figure 1

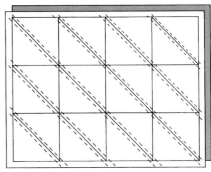

Figure 2

Figure 3

✦ INDIAN TRAILS ✦

This quilt comes from the 1930s, when patchwork was often made from worn cotton dresses and frayed men's shirts. It's a pretty pattern that's easy to piece, and the light pastel colors give it a cool, summery look. Or, for a completely different approach, you might try mixing light and dark colors.

Finished size: Approximately 53 x 59 inches

Materials

Note: Yardages are figured for fabric 45 inches wide.

72 different prints, each 8 x 11 inches (one for
    each block)
1¾ yards solid green fabric
2½ yards bleached muslin
3⅜ yards light blue fabric (backing)
quilt batting 54 x 60 inches
tracing paper
cardboard

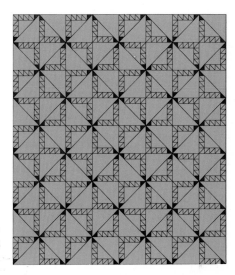

Cutting List

Note: All measurements and patterns include ¼-inch seam allowance. Join all pieces with right sides together, taking ¼-inch seams. Press seams to one side.

Trace patterns A, B and C on page 20 and transfer to cardboard for templates (see page 11).

Cut the following:

from each print:
>   7 A
>   1 B

from green:
>   2 strips, each 2¼ x 50½ inches (for top and bottom borders)
>   2 strips, each 2¼ x 60¼ inches (for side borders)
>   144 A

from muslin:
>   504 A
>   72 C

Directions

To make a block

1. Refer to Figure 1. Stitch a muslin A piece to a print A piece along the diagonal to make a square as shown. Make 7 squares in this way using the same print.

Note: If desired, follow the instructions for right triangles, under Quick-and-Easy Methods on page 14, to make these squares.

2. Refer to Figure 2a. Stitch 3 of these squares together to make a vertical row as shown.

3. Next, stitch the short edge of a green A piece to the bottom edge of the row as shown.

4. Refer to Figure 2b. Stitch the remaining 4 squares together to form a horizontal row as shown. Then stitch the short edge of another green A piece to the right edge of this row as shown.

5. Stitch the vertical row made in steps 1-3 to one short edge of a print B piece as shown in Figure 2c.

6. Refer to Figure 2c and stitch the horizontal row made in step 4 to the other short side of the print B piece to make a large triangle as shown.

7. Refer to Figure 3. Stitch the diagonal edge of the pieced triangle to the diagonal edge of a muslin C piece to make a block as shown. Make 72 blocks in this way.

To make rows

1. Refer to Figure 4a and arrange 8 blocks in a row as shown.

2. Stitch all 8 blocks together to make row 1. Repeat for rows 3, 5, 7 and 9.

3. Refer to Figure 4b and arrange 8 blocks in a row as shown.

4. Stitch all 8 blocks together to make row 2. Repeat for rows 4, 6 and 8.

Figure 1

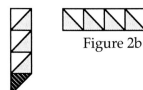

Figure 2b

Figure 2a

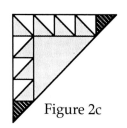

Figure 2c

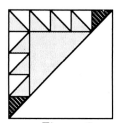

Figure 3

To join rows

1. With right sides together, stitch the bottom edge of row 1 to the top edge of row 2.
2. Next, stitch the bottom edge of row 2 to the top edge of row 3.
3. Continue to join all 9 rows in this way to make the quilt top as shown in Figure 5.

To join borders

1. Join one of the shorter green border strips to the top edge of the quilt top.
2. Repeat with the matching border strip on the bottom edge of the quilt top.
3. Join the remaining border strips to the side edges of the quilt top.

To quilt

Although the quilt shown here was not hand-quilted, you might want to add hand quilting on each white triangle. If so, you should do the following:
1. Trace the feather pattern on page 20 and transfer it to each white triangle on the patchwork quilting top (see page 11).
2. With wrong sides together and batting between, pin the backing, batting and quilt top together.
3. Beginning at the center of the top, take long, loose, basting stitches in a sunburst pattern through all 3 layers.
4. Using small running stitches quilt along the drawn lines on each triangle.
5. When finished remove all basting stitches and pins.

To finish

1. Trim the batting and backing to ¼ inch smaller than the quilt top all around.
2. Turn the raw edges of the borders to the wrong side ¼ inch and press. Then fold the borders over the backing ½ inch all around and press. Pin in place.
3. Machine-stitch or slipstitch the pressed edges in place.

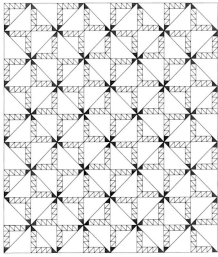

Figure 5

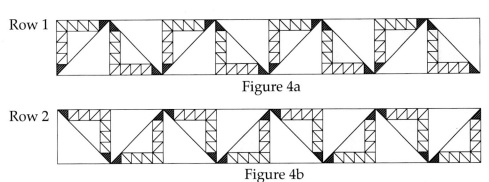

Row 1

Figure 4a

Row 2

Figure 4b

19

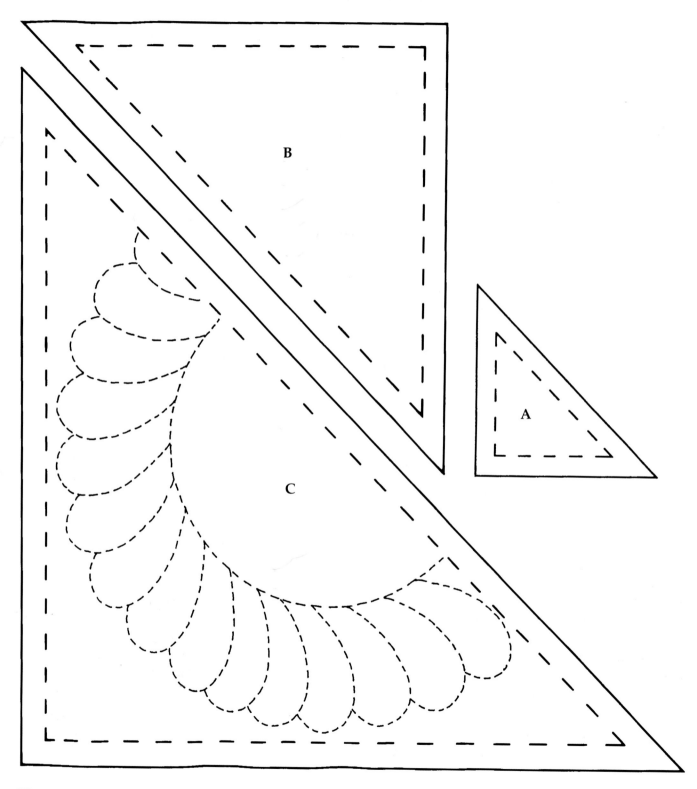

✦ FLOWER GARDEN ✦

One of the popular quilt patterns brought to this country by early English settlers was a one-patch design made from equilateral hexagons. The most familiar is known as Grandmother's Flower Garden, Honeycomb or Mosaic, and there have been many adaptations using different color combinations. The inspiration came from gardens in full bloom. This must have been one of the original projects designed from fabric scraps in a riot of colors and a variety of prints.

This is a challenging quilt to make because there are so many pieces and accuracy is important. Further, the patchwork pieces must be joined by hand. However, it's so pretty that many quilters feel it's worth the effort, especially if they've been collecting fabrics for many years. What makes this particular quilt so pleasing is the use of bright colors on a white background.

Because there are so many (almost 3,500) pieces, I've given the cutting list two different ways: for the entire quilt and then broken down into units so you can cut and stitch sections at different times rather than cutting all the pieces at once.

However, you may prefer to make a smaller quilt or a pillow from just one block. The quilt shown here will fit a double- or queen-size bed.

Finished Size: Approximately 91 x 101 inches

Materials

Note: Yardages are figured for fabric 45 inches wide.

1 yard green fabric

1 yard orange fabric

1 yard yellow fabric

¼ yard each of assorted solid colors other than
    yellow, totaling 3 yards

¼ yard each of assorted prints totaling 2¾
    yards

4½ yards white fabric

8½ yards backing fabric

quilt batting, 91 x 101 inches

freezer paper

11 yards single-fold bias binding

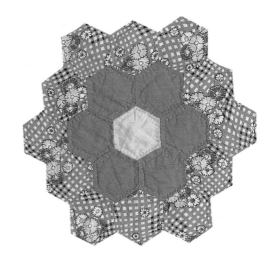

Directions

To make the hexagons

The easiest and most accurate way to make the hundreds of hexagons needed for this project is with freezer paper templates (see page 12).

Place the freezer paper over the hexagon pattern and trace around the outline, which is the size of the finished patchwork piece and does not include seam allowance. Follow the instructions on page 12, adding ¼-inch seam allowance around each hexagon. Prepare at least enough hexagons to make one flower before starting to sew the hexagons together.

You will also need hundreds of white hexagons, which can be made several at a time as you need them to join the motifs.

Cutting List

Cut the following hexagons for the entire quilt:

from prints:
736

from solids:
1100, including yellow for flower centers, plus orange and green from leftover border fabrics

from white:
1186

from orange (border):
222

from green (border):
228

To make flower unit 1

There are 19 hexagons in each flower and 58 flowers on the quilt. Use the template to draw and cut the following to make one flower:

from yellow:
1 hexagon for center

from solids:
6 for the first concentric row

from prints:
12 for the next concentric row

1. Refer to Figure 1a. Beginning with a yellow hexagon for the center of the flower, join a solid hexagon to one edge with small, overcast stitches (see page 9).

2. Refer to Figure 1b. Working clockwise, join another solid hexagon to the next side of the center hexagon, then join the adjacent sides of the 2 solid hexagons. Continue to add the solid hexagons in a concentric circle around the center hexagon in this way.

Figure 1a

Figure 1b

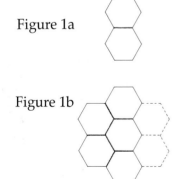

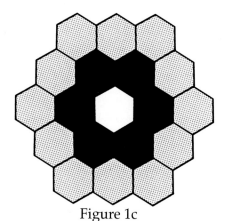

Figure 1c

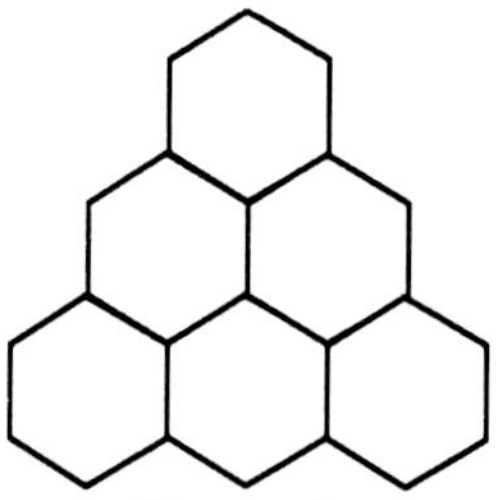

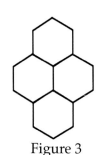

Figure 2

Figure 3

Figure 4

3. Refer to Figure 1c and join the 12 print hexagons in a concentric circle to complete the flower.

4. Make 58 flowers in this way. (Total 1102 hexagons)

To make unit 2

1. Refer to Figure 2. From solids, cut 6 hexagons and arrange as shown.

2. Join together as you did when making the flower units.

3. Make 88 in this way. (Total 528 hexagons)

To make unit 3

1. Refer to Figure 3. From prints, cut 4 hexagons and arrange as shown.

2. Join 2 hexagons along one edge.

3. Continue to join 2 more print hexagons as shown. Make 10 units in this way. (Total 40 hexagons)

To make unit 4

1. Refer to Figure 4. From solids, cut 3 hexagons and arrange as shown.

2. Join 2 hexagons along one edge.

3. Join the third hexagon as shown. Make 26 units in this way. (Total 78 hexagons)

To assemble units

Refer to the color photograph and to Figure 5.

1. Beginning at the top of the quilt, to make row 1, assemble the elements as follows: 6 flowers, 5 of unit 2, 2 of unit 3, 7 of unit 4, and 2 single solid hexagons.

2. Arrange the units and join them with white hexagons as shown.

3. To make row 2, assemble the elements as follows: 7 flowers and 12 of unit 2. Join with white hexagons as shown.

4. To make row 3, assemble the elements as follows: 6 flowers, 10 of unit 2, 2 of unit 3, and 4 of unit 4. Join with white hexagons as shown.

5. Repeat rows 2 and 3 twice more, then repeat row 2 once more and end with a repeat of row 1 in reverse.

6. Make 2 rows of 42 solid hexagons each. Join a white hexagon to each end of each row, then join to the top and bottom of the quilt top as shown in photo.

7. Then, join a row of 43 white hexagons each at the top and bottom of the quilt top.

8. Surround the quilt top with a border of orange hexagons, followed by a border of green hexagons.

To quilt

1. See **Piecing the backing**, page 11. Since this is a very large quilt, you

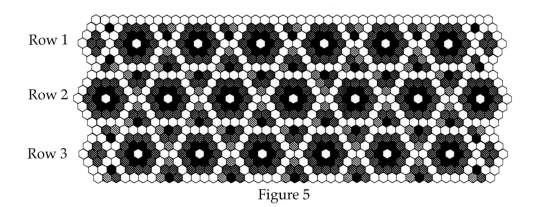

Row 1

Row 2

Row 3

Figure 5

will need one full-width center panel and two narrower panels on each side.

2. Cut quilt batting to same size as the quilt top.

3. With wrong sides together and batting between, pin backing, batting and top together.

4. Beginning at the center and working outward in a sunburst pattern, take long, loose, basting stitches through all 3 layers.

5. Take small running stitches ¼ inch away from all seam lines.

To finish

1. Trim the backing and batting to the same size as the top. Remove basting stitches.

2. Open out one folded edge of bias binding. With right sides together and edges matching, pin one edge of the binding to the quilt top all around. Machine-stitch ¼ inch from edges all around.

3. Fold the binding over to the underside of the quilt and pin all around.

4. Slipstitch the edges in place all around.

FLOWER GARDEN PATTERN

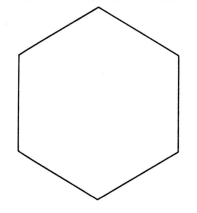

✦ CAROLINA LILY ✦

This is a popular pattern found in many color variations, but I think the combination of bright pink, green and white creates a dramatic design. The flower blocks are made of patchwork, and the stems are appliquéd to the background fabric. Although each block is made from many pattern pieces and is therefore time-consuming, the finished project is worth the effort. The quilting pattern on the pieced blocks is an allover diamond grid, and on the borders a swirl pattern is used.

Finished Size: Approximately 60 x 77 inches

Materials

Note: Yardages are figured for fabric 45 inches wide.

1¾ yards bright pink fabric
2 yards bleached muslin
3 yards green fabric
3½ yards backing fabric
quilt batting, 60 x 77 inches
tracing paper
freezer paper
cardboard

Note: All measurements include ¼-inch seam allowance. Join pieces with right sides together, taking ¼-inch seams. Press seams to one side unless instructed otherwise.

Trace patterns A through K on pages 32-33, transfer to cardboard and cut out for templates (see page 11). Use freezer paper to make templates for the appliqué stems (see next page and page 12).

Cutting List

Cut the following:

from pink:
144 A
6 squares, each 10 x 10 inches
5 squares, each 10⅜ x 10⅜ inches; cut each square on the diagonal to make 10 large triangles.
1 square 10¾ x 10¾ inches; cut on the diagonal in both directions to make 4 small triangles.

from muslin:
> 72 C
> 36 D
> 24 E
> 12 F
> 24 H
> 14 I
> 12 J
> 17 K

from green:
> borders
>> 2 strips, each 5½ x 50½ inches (top and bottom)
>> 2 strips, each 5½ x 77½ inches (sides)
>
> 36 B
> 12 G
> 24 I
> 48 rectangles, each 2¾ x 10 inches (sashing strips)
> 36 appliqué stems (see below)

Directions

To make stem templates

1. Cut freezer paper in ½ x 3-inch strips for templates (see page 12).

2. Using a hot iron press the templates onto the back of the green fabric. Adding ¼-inch seam allowance all around, cut 36 stems. Press the seam allowance on the long edges over the edges of the templates, then peel away the freezer paper, turn the fabric right side up and press again to sharpen the pressed edges. Do not press the short ends under as they will be stitched into the seam allowance when attaching the appliqué squares to the patchwork squares.

To prepare appliqué squares

1. Arrange and pin 3 stems on a muslin F piece as shown on the template.

2. Slipstitch the stems to the muslin piece along the side edges (see page 9). Make 12 in this way and set aside.

To make a block

Refer to Figures 1a-c, 2a-b and 3.

1. Stitch 4 pink A pieces together as shown in Figure 1a.

2. Next, refer to Figure 1b and stitch the diagonal edge of a green B triangle to the bottom edge of the pieced flower as shown. Then, stitch 2 muslin C triangles and 1 muslin D square to the inside corners of the pink A pieces as shown to make a square (see **Sewing inside corner edges**, page 12).

3. Refer to Figure 1c. Stitch one side of each muslin E triangle to two

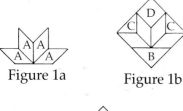

Figure 1a

Figure 1b

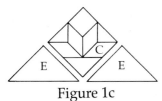

Figure 1c

sides of the square to make a large triangle as shown. This represents the top section of the block.

4. To make 2 more lilies, repeat step 1 two more times.

5. Refer to Figure 2a and assemble the remaining 2 lilies as follows: Join the diagonal edge of a green B triangle to the long edge of this unit as you did in step 2. Then, join 2 muslin C triangles and 1 muslin D piece as shown. Note that the muslin C and D pieces are in a different position than in step 2.

6. Stitch the two lily sections made in steps 4 and 5 to each side edge of one appliquéd F piece as shown.

7. Refer to Figure 2b. Join the long edge of a green G triangle to the bottom edge of the unit made in step 6. This is the bottom section of the block.

8. Stitch the top section of the block to the bottom section.

9. Refer to Figure 3. Stitch one side edge of a green I triangle to one end of a muslin H rectangle. Repeat with another green I triangle and another muslin H rectangle, reversing as shown.

10. Join these two pieces to each side of the block as shown.

11. Join the diagonal edge of a muslin J triangle to the bottom edge of the pieced unit to complete the block as shown.

12. Make 12 blocks in this way.

To make rows

1. Refer to Figure 4a. Stitch the long edge of a green sashing strip to one side edge of a block as shown. Repeat with another green sashing strip on the opposite side edge of the block. Repeat with remaining 11 blocks.

2. For row 1, stitch one side edge of a large pink triangle to the left side edge (green side) of a block as shown. Repeat with another large pink triangle on the opposite side of the block. Refer to Figure 4c and make another in this way for row 6, positioning triangles as shown.

3. Refer to Figure 4b. For row 2, join one side of a large pink triangle to the left side edge of another block in the same way as in step 2 of row 1. Then, join a large pink square, followed by another pieced block, and end with a large pink triangle as shown. Make another for row 5, positioning triangles as shown in Figure 4c.

4. Refer to Figure 4c. Make rows 3 and 4 as shown, using 3 pieced blocks and 2 pink squares and adding a small pink triangle to one end of each row.

Figure 2a

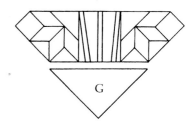

Figure 2b

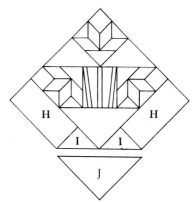

Figure 3

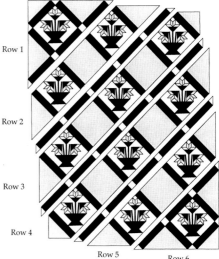

Figure 4c

Figure 4a

Figure 4b

To make row divider strips

1. Refer to Figure 4c. For the top edge of row 1, stitch one side edge of a muslin I triangle to each end of a green sashing strip.
2. Stitch another muslin I triangle to the left-hand end of another green sashing strip. Then stitch a muslin K square to the right-hand end of that strip, followed by another green strip, then another muslin square and another green strip, and end with a muslin I triangle. This strip will join rows 1 and 2.
3. Continue to make all 7 row divider strips as shown in Figure 4c.

To join rows

1. Refer to Figure 4c. Join the bottom edge of the first row divider strip to the top edge of row 1.
2. Next, join the diagonal edge of a small pink triangle to the top edge of the first divider strip.
3. Join the bottom edge of row 1 to the top edge of the second row divider strip. Then stitch the bottom edge of the second divider strip to the top edge of row 2.
4. Continue to join all 6 rows with row divider strips as shown.
5. With right sides together, join the diagonal edge of the last small pink triangle to the bottom edge of the last row divider strip to complete the quilt top.

To join borders

1. Join one short border strip to the top edge of the quilt top. Repeat on the bottom edge.
2. Join the remaining border strips to the side edges of the quilt top.

To prepare for quilting

1. Cut backing fabric in half crosswise. Then follow the instructions for piecing the backing, page 11.
2. Trace and transfer the quilting pattern to the borders of the quilt top (see page 11).
3. Measure and mark a 1-inch grid pattern on all the pink squares and triangles (see page 13).

To quilt

1. With wrong sides together and batting between, pin the quilt top, batting and backing fabric together.
2. Beginning at the center and working outward in a sunburst pattern, take long, loose basting stitches through all 3 layers.
3. Using small running stitches quilt on all pre-marked lines.

To finish

1. When all quilting is complete, remove basting stitches.
2. Cut batting ¼ inch smaller than quilt top all around.
3. Trim backing fabric to same size as quilt top all around.
4. Turn the raw edges of the quilt top and backing to the wrong side ¼ inch and press.
5. Machine-stitch or slipstitch the pressed edges together all around.

Cable Quilting Pattern for Borders

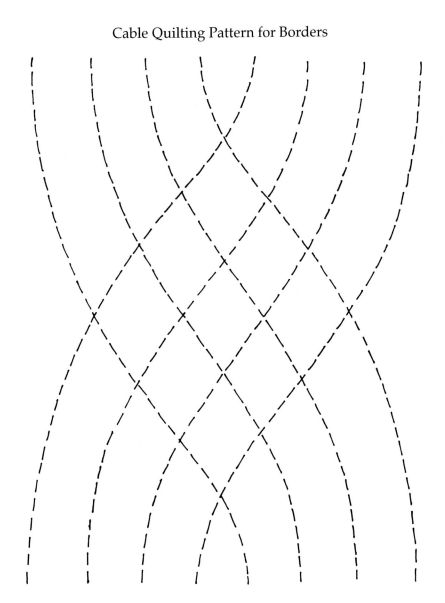

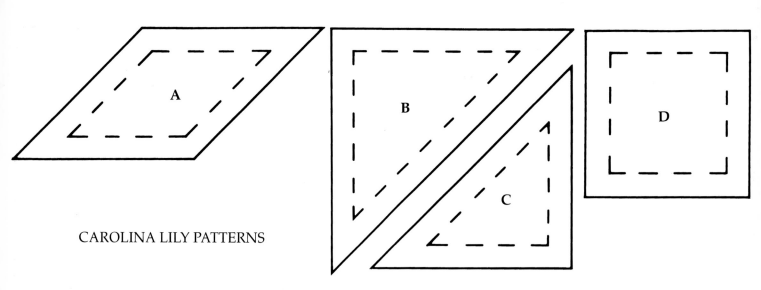

CAROLINA LILY PATTERNS

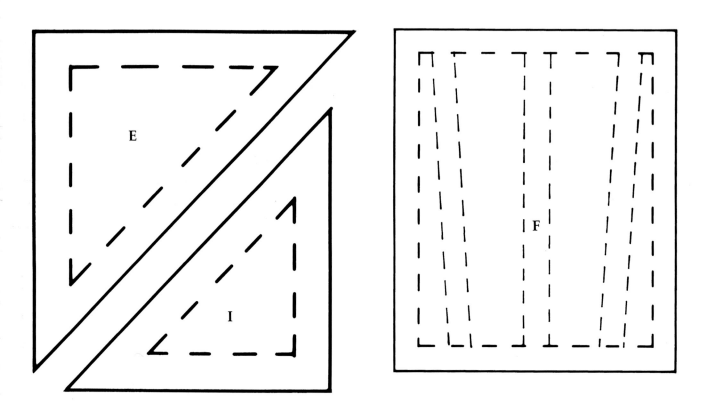

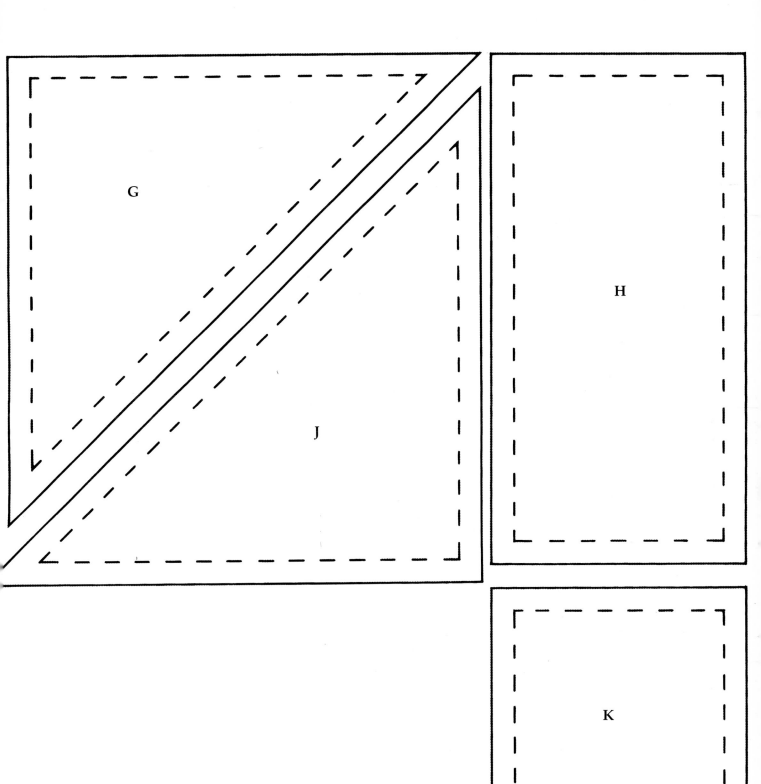

G

J

H

K

WORD ✦ WITHOUT END ✦

The fabrics for this quilt are typical of the colors and prints of the 1930s. The pattern is sometimes called Kaleidoscope, and it has a playful, circus-like quality. It is one of many early quilt patterns that can be made from fabric scraps, and the more lively the colors and prints the better. The patchwork motifs are first pieced and then appliquéd to individual muslin squares. This would make a nice quilt for a child's room.

Finished Size: Approximately 70½ x 70½ inches

Materials

Note: Yardages are figured for fabric 45 inches wide.

a variety of print scraps
¼ yard each of 5 different solid colors
3¾ yards muslin
4¼ yards print fabric for backing
quilt batting, 71 x 71 inches
tracing paper
cardboard
embroidery floss and embroidery needle (optional)

Note: All templates and measurements include ¼-inch seam allowance. Join pieces with right sides together, taking ¼-inch seams. Press seams to one side unless instructed otherwise.

Trace patterns A and B and transfer to cardboard to make templates (see page 11). Trace around the templates on the wrong side of the fabric and cut out as indicated below.

Cutting List

Cut the following:
from assorted scraps:
    400 A
from solids:
    100 B (20 of each color)
from muslin:
    25 squares, each 14½ x 14½ inches

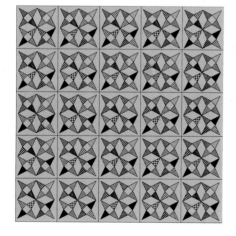

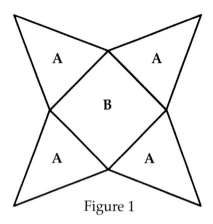

Figure 1

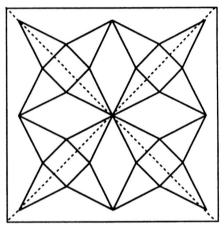

Figure 2

Directions

To make a block

1. Refer to Figure 1. Stitch the short edge of a print A piece to one edge of a solid B square as shown.
2. Continue to join 3 more A pieces to the edges of the B square as shown.
3. Turn the seam allowances on the raw edges of the A pieces under and press.
4. Using the same color B square in the center, make 3 more pieced units in this way.
5. Finger-press a muslin square on the diagonal in each direction to create an X guide for placement of the patchwork pieces.
6. Refer to Figure 2. Position the 4 patchwork units on the muslin square so the points meet in the center. Pin in position.
7. Using an overcast stitch or slipstitch (see page 9), sew the pressed edges of the appliqué in place. If you'd like to add a decorative touch you can work blanket stitch (page 9) around the edges using coordinating embroidery floss.
8. Make 25 blocks in this way.

To make rows

1. Refer to Figure 3. Join 2 appliqué blocks along one side edge.
2. Continue to join 3 more blocks in this way to complete row 1.
3. Make 5 rows of 5 blocks each.

Figure 3

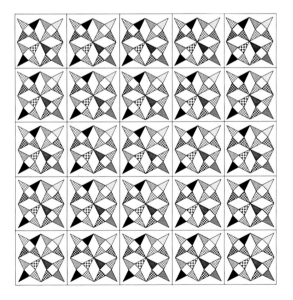

To join rows

1. Refer to Figure 3. With right sides together and seams aligned, join the bottom edge of row 1 to the top edge of row 2.
2. Join remaining rows in this way.

To prepare for quilting

1. Cut the backing fabric in half crosswise. Then follow the instructions for piecing the backing on page 11.
2. With wrong sides together and batting between, pin the backing, batting and top together.
3. Beginning at the center and working outward in a sunburst pattern, take long, loose basting stitches through all 3 layers.

To tie-quilt

1. Refer to page 14 and tie the quilt through all layers at each intersection of the muslin blocks.
2. If you prefer to hand-quilt, take small running stitches ¼ inch away from the outside edges of each appliqué in each block.

To finish

1. When all quilting is complete, remove basting stitches.
2. Trim the batting to the same size as the quilt top all around.
3. Trim the backing to 1 inch larger than the quilt top all around.
4. Turn the raw edges of the backing forward ¼ inch and press. Then bring the remaining backing fabric forward onto the quilt top and pin all around.
5. Slipstitch the pressed edges in place.

WORLD WITHOUT END PATTERNS

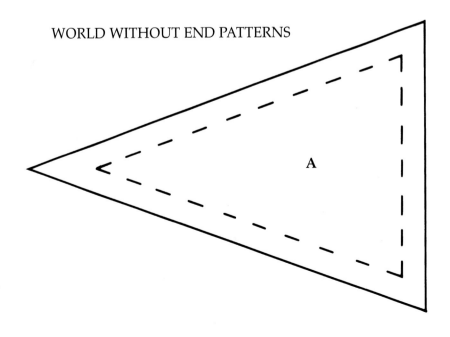

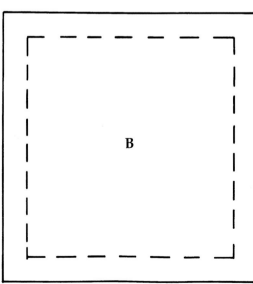

✦ SUNFLOWER ✦

Numerous versions of this pattern have emerged over the years, each with a different name. However, all interpretations seem to evoke images of a field of flowers. The pattern is similar to the Dresden Plate (see page 120) and is pieced in the same way. Typically, this quilt is made from scraps of fabrics taken from old clothing or left over from other sewing projects.

Finished Size: 74 x 91 inches

Materials

Note: Yardages are figured for fabric 45 inches wide.

a variety of assorted print fabrics
½ yard yellow fabric
6½ yards muslin
5¼ yards backing fabric
quilt batting, 74 x 91 inches
tracing paper
cardboard

Cutting List

Note: All measurements include ¼-inch seam allowance. Join all pieces with right sides together, taking ¼-inch seams. Press seams to one side.

Trace patterns A and B and transfer to cardboard to make templates (see page 11). Pattern A includes seam allowances. Pattern B is for an appliqué. Trace it onto the wrong side of the fabric as indicated below and, when cutting out the fabric, add ¼-inch seam allowance all around.

Cut the following:
from print scraps:
    450 A

from yellow:
    20 B

from muslin:
    2 strips, each 3½ x 68½ inches (for top and bottom borders)
    2 strips, each 3½ x 91½ inches (for side borders)
    20 squares, each 17½ x 17½ inches

Figure 1a

Figure 1b

Figure 1c

Figure 2

Directions

To make a block

1. Refer to Figure 1a. With right sides together, stitch 2 A pieces together along one straight edge as shown.
2. Refer to Figure 1b and continue to join 18 A pieces in this way to form the sunflower petals.
3. Turn under the seam allowances on the raw edges of each side of the points and press.
4. Center the sunflower petals on a muslin square and pin in position.
5. Center template B on the wrong side of a yellow fabric circle and clip into the seam allowance all around. Using a hot iron, press the seam allowance over the edge of the template.
6. Remove the template and place the yellow circle right side up over the center of the petals on the muslin square as shown in Figure 1c. Pin in place.
7. Using an overcast stitch or slipstitch (see page 9), sew the appliqué to the muslin background fabric along all turned edges of the petals and the center circle to complete the block.
8. Make 20 blocks in this way.

To make rows

1. Join 2 appliqué blocks along one side edge.
2. Continue to join 2 more blocks in this way to complete row 1.
3. Make 5 rows of 4 blocks each.

To join rows

1. Refer to Figure 2. With seams aligned, join the bottom edge of row 1 to the top edge of row 2.
2. Continue to join all 5 rows in this way.

To make borders

1. Join one short border strip to the top edge of the quilt top.
2. Repeat on the bottom edge of the quilt top.
3. Join the remaining border strips to the side edges of the quilt top in the same way.

To quilt

This project was quilted in a series of concentric circles over each block. However, it might be prettier and easier to follow the lines of the sunflowers and quilt ¼ inch away from the outside edges of each appliqué.

If you prefer to quilt in circles, use a compass to mark concentric circles ½ inch apart from the center of the edge of each block.

1. Cut the backing fabric in half crosswise. Then follow the instructions for piecing the backing on page 11.

2. With wrong sides together and batting between, pin the backing, batting and quilt top together.

3. Beginning at the center and working outward in a sunburst pattern, take long, loose basting stitches through all 3 layers.

4. Using small running stitches, quilt along all pre-marked circles (or ¼ inch away from the outside edge of each appliqué in each block). Quilt ¼ inch from each side of the border seamlines as well. Do not stitch into the seam allowance around the edge of the quilt.

To finish

1. When all quilting is complete, remove basting stitches.
2. Trim the batting to ¼ inch smaller than the quilt top all around.
3. Trim the backing to the same size as the quilt top.
4. Turn the raw edges of the quilt top and the backing to the wrong side ¼ inch and press.
5. Machine-stitch or slipstitch the pressed edges together all around.

SUNFLOWER PATTERNS

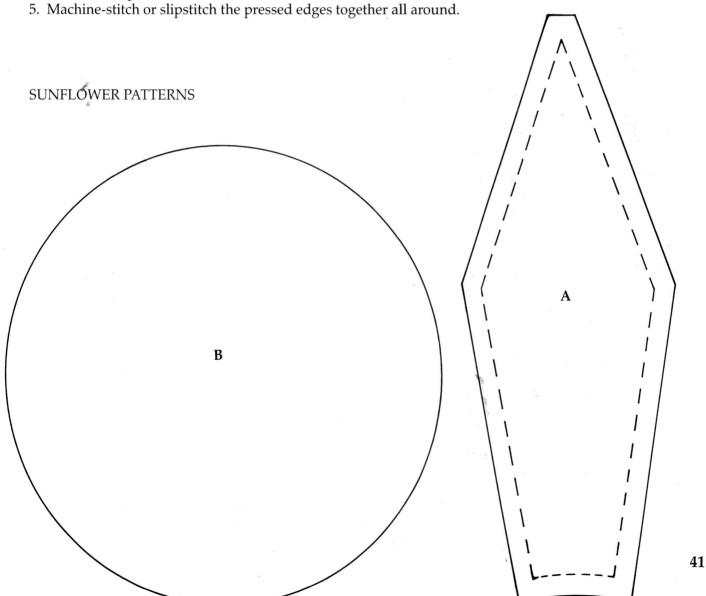

✦ FLOWER BASKET ✦

The pattern for an appliquéd basket of flowers as the central motif of a quilt was being offered in popular women's magazines as early as 1915. This design was also a favorite with commercial pattern makers. By the 1930s there must have been hundreds of quilts made from stamped patterns of a woven basket holding a variety of colorful fabric flowers.

Each large flower on this vintage quilt was made with an appliqué called a yo-yo, an individual round piece of fabric gathered in the center, then sewn to the background. The delicate bow on the basket is especially pretty. Note that this project is assembled and quilted first, then appliquéd.

Finished Size: 72 x 88 inches

Materials

Note: Yardages are figured for fabric 45 inches wide.

¼ yard each of the following colors: red, pink,
    light and dark rose, light and dark purple,
    light and medium gray, pale yellow,
    light and medium gold, bright blue, and
    dark green fabric
½ yard each pale blue, medium green, and tan
    fabric
5½ yards off-white fabric
7 yards lavender fabric (includes backing)
quilt batting, 72 x 88 inches
tracing paper
freezer paper
cardboard
pearl cotton for embroidery and embroidery
    needle

Note: Measurements for all quilt panels and borders and bias strips for stems and basket, and pattern for yo-yo, include ¼-inch seam allowance. Join pieces with right sides together, taking ¼-inch seams. Press seams to one side unless instructed otherwise. Cut bias strips as instructed below (they are ¼ inch wide when folded). Trace the yo-yo pattern on page 50 and transfer to cardboard to make a template (see page 11). Trace remaining pattern pieces on pages 49 and 52-53 (which

Figure 1

do not include seam allowance) onto freezer paper for templates (see page 12). When cutting pieces from freezer paper templates, add ¼-inch seam allowance all around. Refer to Figure 1, Assembly Guide (page 47), and color photograph for position of pieces.

Cutting List

Cut the following:

from off-white:
    2 strips, each 11½ x 50½ inches (outside border, top and bottom)
    2 strips, each 11½ x 88½ inches (outside border, sides)
    1 piece, 34½ x 50½ inches (center panel)

from lavender:

 2 strips, each 8½ x 34½ inches (inside border, top and bottom)
 2 strips, each 8½ x 66½ inches (inside border, sides)

from all colors except red, green, tan and pale blue:

 34 yo-yos

from medium green:

 ¾-inch wide bias strips, cut as follows for all stem pieces except bell
  flower stems and 2 heart flower stems (see Figure 1):
  8 A, each 8 inches long
  2 B, each 11½ inches long
  1 C, 13½ inches long
  3 D, each 2¼ inches long
  1 E, 1¾ inches long
  1 F, 17½ inches long
  65 leaf pieces

from medium gray:

 5 bell flowers

from dark green:

 ¾-inch wide bias strips, cut as follows for stems for bell flowers and
  2 heart flowers on left side of motif:
 1 G, 4¼ inches long
 1 H, 2¼ inches long
 4 I, each 2 inches long

from dark rose:

 7 heart-shaped flowers (1 small, 2 medium, 4 large)

from pale blue:

 bow sections (cut pieces 1 through 7, then cut pieces 1 through 6 in
  reverse)

from tan:

 ¾-inch wide bias strips, cut as follows for all basket pieces:
  2 J, each 23¼ inches long
  1 K, 14 inches long (fold miters into bottom corners of basket)
  1 strip approximately 40 inches long, for weaving basket:
   Following Figure 1 for placement, cut this strip into 9 pieces
   trimmed as needed.

Directions

To make yo-yos

1. Refer to Figures 2a and 2b. Turn under ¼-inch seam allowance around the outside edge of all round fabric pieces and press.
2. Using doubled thread, hand-sew a small running stitch around the circle next to the folded edge, gather tightly and secure the thread.
3. Flatten the yo-yo, centering the gathered hole; press. Make 34 in this way.

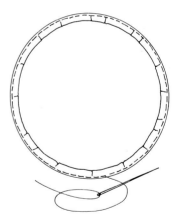

Figure 2a

Figure 2b

To prepare appliqué pieces

See **Freezer paper templates**, page 12, and **Spring Tulips For The Bedroom**, page 67, to prepare each appliqué piece. For stems and basket pieces, cut bias strips to the dimensions given in Cutting List. To shape, first press long edges ¼ inch to wrong side; then shape and press the strips into the curves indicated in Figure 1. When assembling the design, slip the raw ends under flowers or intersecting pieces, turning under to finish if necessary.

Note: If desired, stems and basket pieces may be made from double-fold bias tape.

To make quilt top

1. Refer to Assembly Guide (page 47). Join an 8½ x 34½-inch lavender strip to the top edge of the off-white center panel. Press these and all similar seams to the lavender side.
2. Repeat on the bottom edge of the center panel.
3. Join the remaining lavender strips to the side edges in the same way.
4. Join an 11½ x 50½-inch off-white strip to the top edge of the lavender strip.
5. Repeat on the bottom edge of the quilt top.
6. Join the remaining off-white strips to each side edge of the quilt top.

To prepare for quilting

1. Refer to Figure 3. Trace and transfer the feather quilting pattern to each corner of the center panel, reversing as necessary.
2. Refer to Figure 3. Trace and transfer the inside border pattern around the lavender inside border.
3. Trace and transfer the petal design to create a rosette in each corner of the lavender inside border (see Figure 3).
4. Trace and transfer the fish-scale design to the off-white outside border strips (see Figure 3).
5. Starting at one corner of the center panel and working on the diagonal, measure and mark all previously unmarked areas with lines 1 inch apart to the opposite corner. Repeat in the opposite direction to create a diamond grid over the center panel. Mark the borders in the same way.
6. For the backing, cut the remaining lavender fabric in half crosswise. Then follow the instructions for piecing the backing on page 11.

To quilt

1. With wrong sides together and batting between, pin the top, batting and backing together.
2. Beginning in the center and working outward in a sunburst pattern, take long, loose, basting stitches through all 3 layers.
3. Using small running stitches, quilt along all pre-marked lines.

Figure 3

To apply appliqués

1. Referring to Figure 1 and Assembly Guide, position and pin each appliqué piece, including the yo-yos, in position on the quilt top.

2. Sew each appliqué piece in place using an overcast stitch or slip-stitch (page 9) around all turned edges.

To finish

1. Trim the batting to the same size as the quilt top.

2. Trim the backing fabric to 1 inch larger than the quilt top all around.

3. Turn the backing fabric forward ¼ inch and press.

4. Turn the remaining fabric forward onto the quilt top and pin all around.

5. Slipstitch pressed edges in place.

6. Using contrasting pearl cotton, work several long straight stitches, crisscrossing the center hole of each yo-yo flower.

Assembly Guide

FLOWER BASKET QUILTING PATTERNS

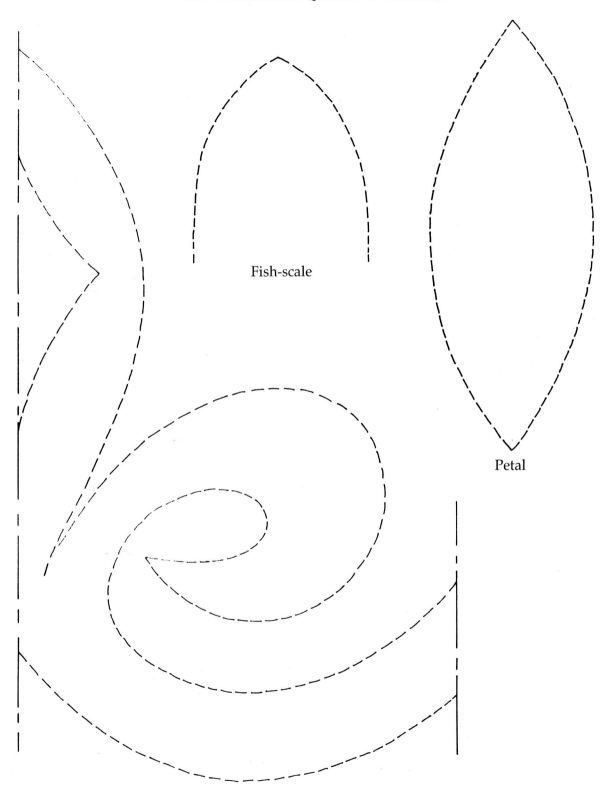

Fish-scale

Petal

FLOWER BASKET APPLIQUÉ PATTERNS

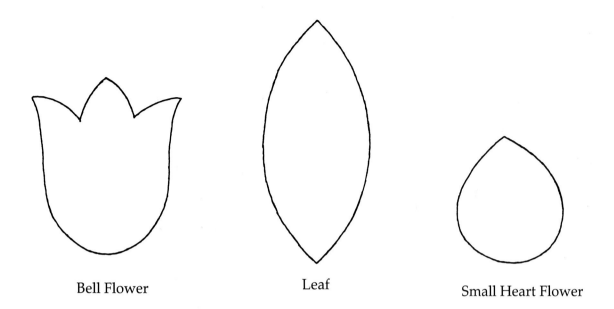

Bell Flower

Leaf

Small Heart Flower

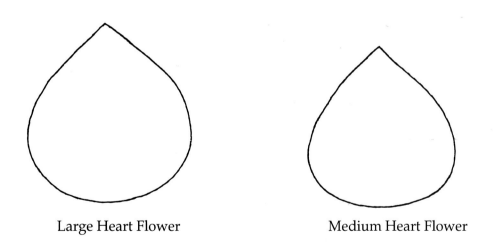

Large Heart Flower

Medium Heart Flower

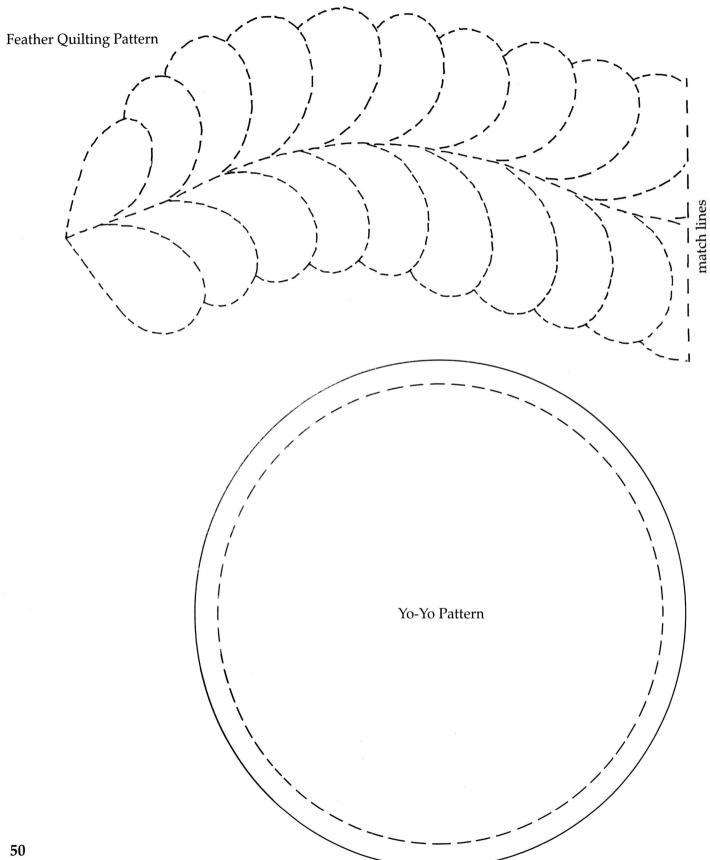

Feather Quilting Pattern

match lines

Yo-Yo Pattern

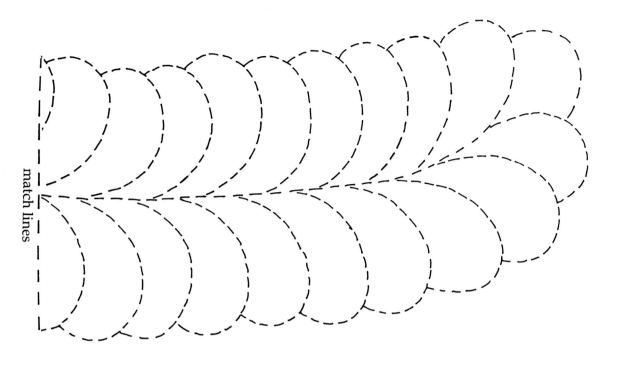

match lines

51

FLOWER BASKET APPLIQUÉ PATTERNS

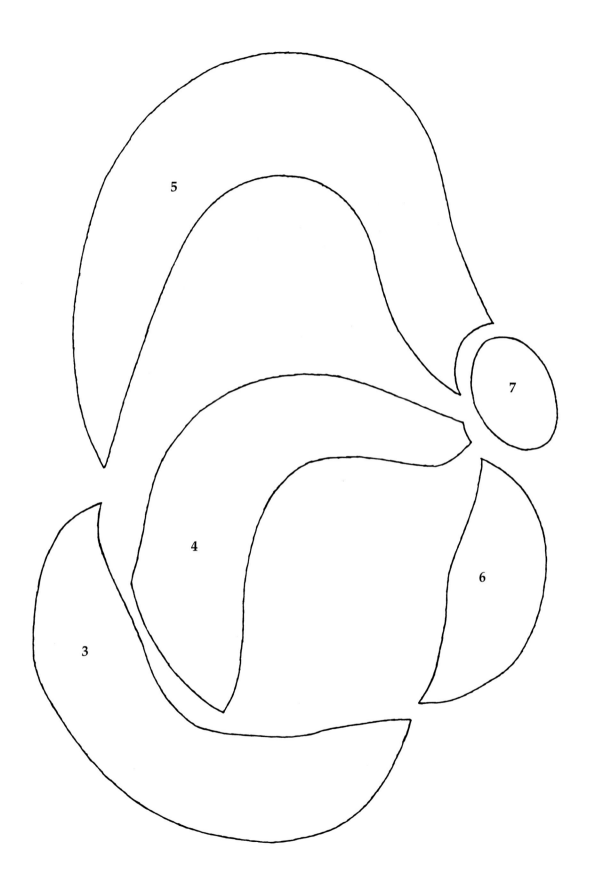

LADY FROM PETTICOAT ROW

◆ ◆

This colonial-lady pattern became popular in the 1920s and was often featured in magazines such as *Ladies' Home Journal*, as well as being offered in kit form. It provided an opportunity to use up colorful scraps of fabric and to combine patchwork, appliqué and embroidery. Each block measures 16 x 16 inches. The quilt shown here was quilted by machine in an allover scroll pattern. A good alternative is hand or machine quilting in an allover diamond grid pattern (see **Allover quilting**, page 13). Or follow the instructions given below to quilt along the seamlines.

Finished Size: Approximately 66 x 87 inches

Materials

Note: Yardages are figured for fabric 45 inches wide.

⅓ yard each of 12 different prints
2¾ yards yellow fabric
¼ yard gray fabric
7¾ yards muslin (includes backing)
1 skein each black, orange, and yellow
    embroidery floss
embroidery needle
quilt batting, 66 x 87 inches
tracing paper
thin cardboard

Note: All measurements include ¼-inch seam allowance. Join pieces with right sides together, taking ¼-inch seams. Press seams to one side unless instructed otherwise.

Trace pattern pieces A through H on pages 59-60. Transfer onto cardboard to make templates (see page 11). When cutting out each fabric piece add a ¼-inch seam allowance all around except where it has been added to the pattern as indicated by a broken line.

Cutting List

Cut the following:
from muslin:
    12 squares, each 16½ x 16½ inches

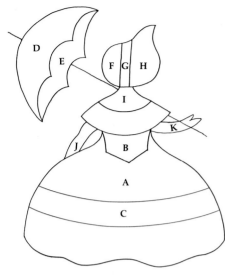

Figure 1

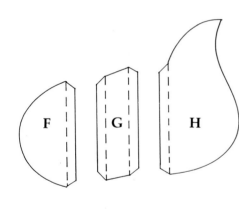

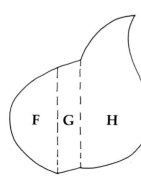

Figure 2

from yellow:

    6 strips, each 4½ x 16½ inches

    9 strips, each 5½ x 16½ inches

    2 strips, each 4½ x 87½ inches for side borders

    2 strips, each 5½ x 87½ inches for vertical dividers

    12 each of B, C, E and F

from assorted prints:

    12 each of A, D and H

from gray:

    12 each of G

Directions

To make appliqué squares

1. Place each template on the wrong side of the corresponding fabric and clip into the seam allowance on all curved edges. Then, press the seam allowances over the edges of the template all around.

2. Remove the template, turn the fabric over and press again to sharpen the pressed edges.

3. Refer to Figure 1. Pin each appliqué piece to center of muslin square in alphabetical order, A through E.

4. Sew in place using an overcast stitch or slipstitch (page 9).

5. Trace embroidery patterns I, J and K and transfer in position to the muslin square (see page 12).

6. Separate the 6 strands of embroidery floss into groups of 3 strands. Using stem/outline stitch (page 9), embroider the outline of shoulders and arms in orange and the umbrella shaft in black and yellow.

7. Refer to Figure 2. To assemble the bonnet, join the straight edge of piece F to the adjacent edge of G, then join H.

8. Pin and sew bonnet appliqué in place. Using a running stitch (page 9), outline pieces A through H in black.

9. Make 12 appliqué blocks in this way.

Note: To make a placement guide for the appliqués, arrange the templates and embroidery-guide patterns as shown in Figure 1, then center a 16½-inch square piece of tracing paper over them and trace all lines onto it. To arrange the appliqués, place the tracing over each muslin square, pin along the top edge, and slide the pieces into position under it.

To make vertical rows

1. Refer to Figure 3. Join a 4½ x 16½-inch yellow strip to the top edge of an appliqué square. Press this and all similar seams to the yellow side.

2. Join a 5½ x 16½-inch yellow strip to the bottom edge of this appliqué square.

3. Add another appliqué square to the bottom edge of the yellow strip, followed by another 5½ x 16½-inch yellow strip, an appliqué square, another 5½ x 16½-inch yellow strip, another appliqué square, and end with a 4½ x 16½-inch yellow strip on the bottom edge of the last square.

4. Make 2 more rows in this way.

To join rows

1. Refer to Figure 4. Join a 5½ x 87½-inch yellow strip to the right-hand long edge of row 1.

2. Next, join row 2 to the opposite long edge of the yellow strip in the same way.

3. Join the other long edge of row 2 to one long edge of the remaining 5½ x 87½-inch strip.

4. Join row 3 to the raw edge of the yellow strip.

To join side borders

Join the remaining yellow strips to the side edges of the quilt top (see Figure 4).

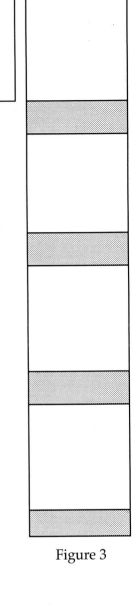

Figure 3

Row 1   Row 2   Row 3

Figure 4

To quilt

1. Cut the remaining muslin fabric in half crosswise. Then follow the instructions for piecing the backing on page 11.
2. With wrong sides together and batting between, pin the backing, batting and top together.
3. Beginning at the center and working outward in a sunburst pattern, take long, loose, basting stitches through all 3 layers.
4. Take small running stitches along all seamlines of yellow strips, stopping short of the seam allowance around the outside edges of the quilt.

To finish

1. When all quilting is complete, remove basting stitches.
2. Trim the batting to ¼ inch smaller than the quilt top all around.
3. Trim the backing to the same size as the quilt top.
4. Turn the raw edges of the backing and the quilt top to the wrong side ¼ inch and press.
5. Machine-stitch as close as possible to the outside edge all around.

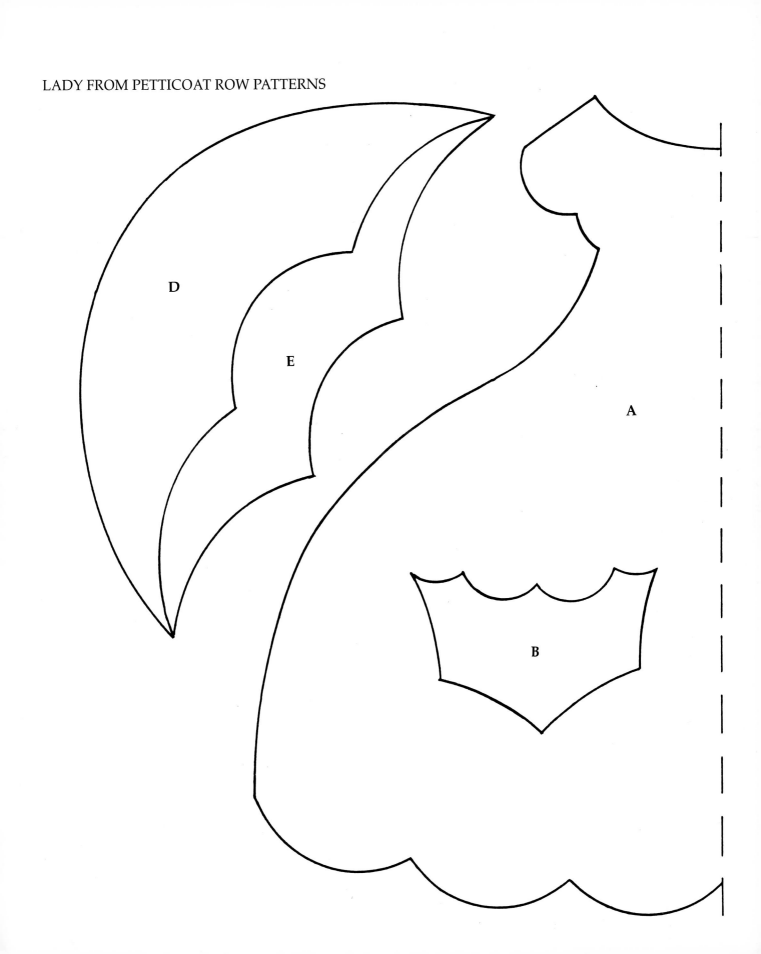

LADY FROM PETTICOAT ROW PATTERNS

D

E

A

B

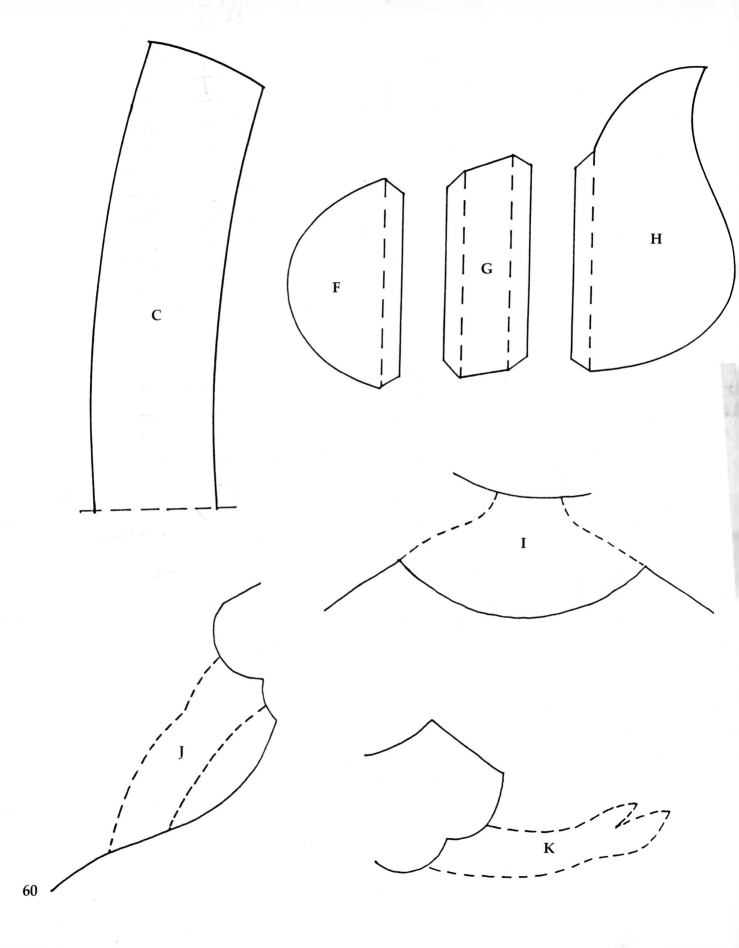

C

F

G

H

I

J

60

K

♦ OVERALL SAM ♦
TOY BOX

During the Depression quiltmaking became quite popular, both as a diversion and as a way to save money. Many of the designs were provided by the women's magazines of the time. One design that caught on and is still popular today was Sunbonnet Sue and Overall Sam, two childlike figures wearing enormous hats that covered their faces. These charming characters were easy appliqués to create and were usually applied to the background fabric with a decorative embroidery stitch. Details on the clothing were also done with embroidery, another popular craft at the time.

This motif can be applied to a muslin background for use as a wall-hanging or quilt, a framed picture to hang in a child's room, or, as shown here, to cover a padded seat on a wooden toy box. (See page 131 for another version of this project.)

Finished Size: 14 x 17 inches or to fit your box

Materials

Note: Yardages are figured for fabric 45 inches wide.

½ yard muslin
1 yard peach fabric
7 x 9-inch piece of print fabric
1 skein black embroidery floss

embroidery needle
toy box
½ yard quilt batting or foam rubber to fit
    top of toy box
staple gun

Cutting List

Trace all pattern pieces including the embroidery details. Transfer the details in position on each fabric piece (see page 11). (If you can see through your fabric, you can place the fabric over the pattern and trace right onto the fabric.) Do not add seam allowances.

Cut the following:

from print:
    1 main body pattern piece
    2 flower pattern pieces

from peach:
    1 hat pattern piece
    1 each of the foot pattern pieces

from muslin:
    1 piece, 17 x 18 inches

Figure 1

Directions

To make appliqué

1. On each 18-inch edge of muslin press under ¼ inch, then ½ inch. Stitch hems in place. Do not hem other edges.

2. Refer to Figure 1. Arrange the appliqué pieces on the center of the muslin fabric. Pin pieces so the edge of the hat overlaps the top edge of the body and the bottom edge of the body overlaps the top edge of each foot as shown. Pin flowers in place as shown in photo.

3. Separate the 6 strands of embroidery floss and, using only 3 strands, work blanket stitch (see page 9) around body, hat and feet to apply appliqué to the muslin background. Apply flowers in same way.

4. Using 3 strands of embroidery floss use stem/outline stitch (see page 9) to create the transferred details on the body, hat and flowers.

To finish

1. For padding, cut the quilt batting (use a double layer if desired) to fit the top of the box, or place the foam rubber on the box top.

2. Next, wrap the top and sides with the peach fabric and staple the edges under the lid. Trim away any excess fabric.

3. Center the appliquéd muslin piece over the peach fabric, pull it taut, and staple the top and bottom edges under the lid.

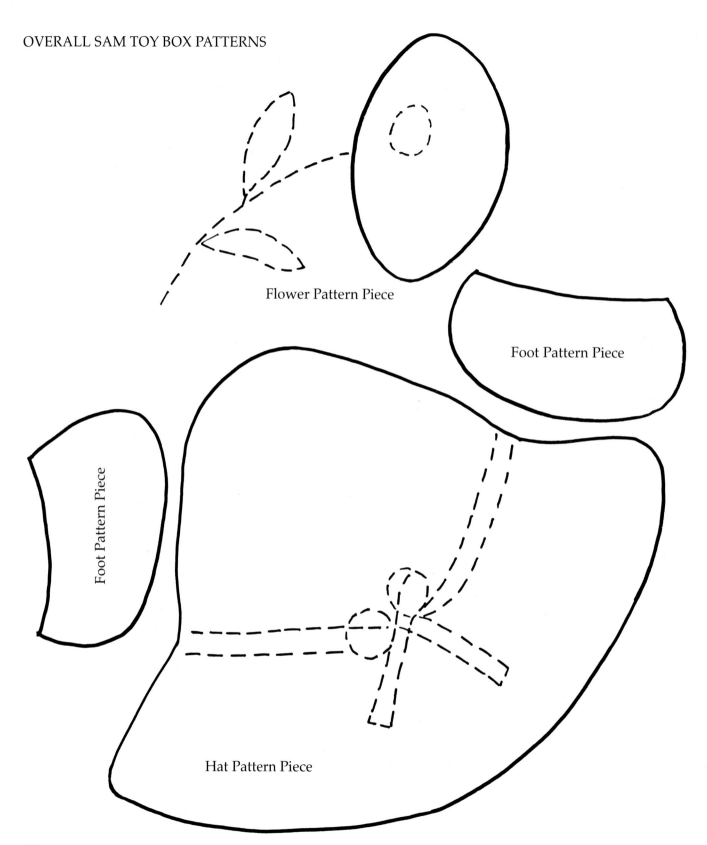

Flower Pattern Piece

Foot Pattern Piece

Foot Pattern Piece

Hat Pattern Piece

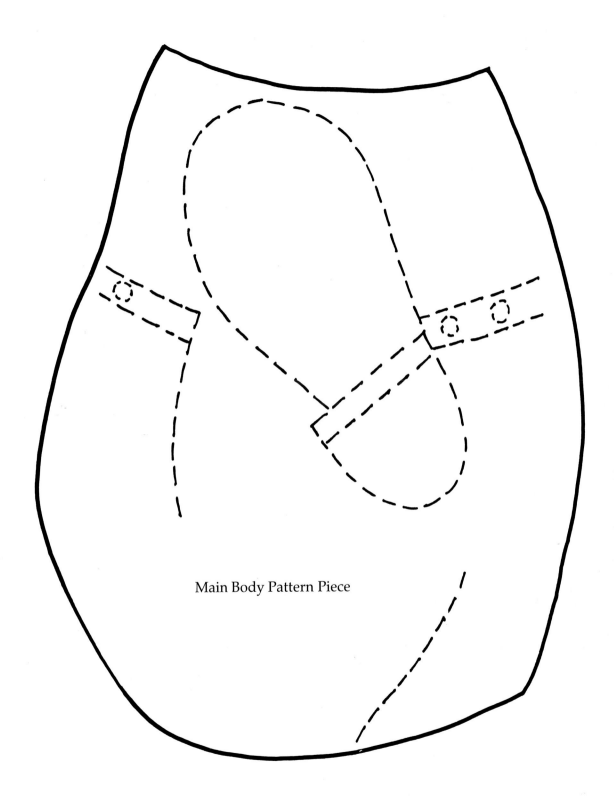

Main Body Pattern Piece

✦ SPRING TULIPS ✦ FOR THE BEDROOM

Tulips have been interpreted in many ways for both appliquéd and pieced quilts. In Scandinavia, red tulips are associated with Christmas, but traditionally the tulip has been created with pastel colors for bedroom quilts. The use of soft yellow, pink, lavender and green on a white background is fresh and light for a bedroom ensemble. I adapted the motif of this 1930s quilt to create a matching pillow and window valance for a coordinated decor.

The pillow is made as for a single appliqué block from the quilt. For the valance I used four evenly spaced appliqués on muslin, which I then stapled to a padded wooden valance made to fit the window. Note that the tulip appliqué on the valance is a variation of those on the quilt and pillow.

Quilt

Finished Size: 80 x 80 inches

Materials

Note: Yardages are figured for fabric 45 inches wide.

1 yard green fabric
¼ yard yellow fabric
¼ yard lavender fabric
¼ yard pink fabric
6¾ yards white
4½ yards muslin or other fabric for backing
quilt batting
freezer paper

Note: All measurements include ¼-inch seam allowance. Join pieces with right sides together, taking ¼-inch seams. Press seams to one side unless instructed otherwise.

To cut templates

I recommend the freezer paper method for making templates for this project (see page 12). However, you can cut templates from cardboard if you prefer (see page 11).

1. Place the freezer paper over pattern pieces A and B (all patterns are on page 74) and trace and cut out the number indicated for each fabric color in the Cutting List, below.

2. For the curved stems: Place the freezer paper over pattern piece D and trace, then complete the stem by tracing pattern C as an extension of D with the broken lines matching. Turn this tracing over to make another template in the same way but curving to the right. These are the stems for the left and right tulips.

3. Next, follow the same procedure and trace pattern pieces E and F to make the long stem for the center tulip.

4. Place the shiny side of each template on the wrong side of the fabrics indicated below and press with a hot iron. The paper will adhere temporarily.

5. When cutting out each piece of fabric, add ¼-inch seam allowance all around. Then clip into the seam allowance around each piece and press the edges over onto the template.

6. Peel away the paper, turn the fabric over and press again. Prepare all template pieces in this way.

Note: If desired, instead of cutting templates, stems may be made from purchased single-fold bias tape. For center stems, cut pieces 16½ inches long (13); for side stems, cut pieces 12 inches long (26). Shape the side stems with a medium hot iron, curving them as you press.

Cutting List

Cut the following:

from yellow:
    13 A

from lavender:
    13 A

from pink:
    13 A

from green:
    52 B
    26 C/D
    13 E/F

from white:
    2 strips, each 5½ x 70½ inches (for side borders)
    2 strips, each 5½ x 80½ inches (for top and bottom borders)
    13 squares, each 17 x 17 inches
    4 squares, each 17⅜ x 17⅜ inches; cut each square in half diagonally to make 2 triangles each (8 large triangles)
    1 square, 17¾ x 17¾ inches; cut on the diagonal in each direction to make 4 small triangles

To make a block

1. Refer to Figure 1. Starting at the bottom edge of one corner of a white square, position and pin the long center stem.
2. Next, pin a curved stem on either side of the center stem.
3. Position and pin a leaf at each side of the center stem, approximately 3 inches from the top of the stem, and pin a leaf at each outside edge of the curved stems, approximately 4 inches from the top of the stems.
4. Position and pin a lavender tulip over the top edge of the center stem, a yellow tulip over the right stem and a pink tulip over the left stem.
5. Using an overcast stitch or slipstitch (see page 9), sew the turned edges of each appliqué piece to the background fabric. Make 13 squares in this way.

Figure 1

To make rows

1. Refer to Figure 2. For row 1, join one short edge of a large white triangle to the left side edge of an appliqué block.
2. Repeat with another large triangle on the right side edge of the block as shown.
3. Join the diagonal edge of a small white triangle to the top edge of the appliqué block as shown.
4. To make row 2, join a large white triangle to an appliqué block, then join 2 more appliqué blocks and end the row with another large white triangle as shown. Repeat for row 4, positioning triangles as shown.
5. For row 3, join the diagonal edge of a small white triangle to the left side edge of a block. Then, join 4 more blocks and end with a small white triangle as shown.
6. For row 5, join a large white triangle to a block, and then join another large white triangle as shown. Join the diagonal edge of the remaining small white triangle to the remaining raw edge of the block.

To join rows

1. Refer to Figures 2 and 3. With seams aligned, join the bottom edge of row 1 to the top edge of row 2.
2. Continue to join all rows in this way.

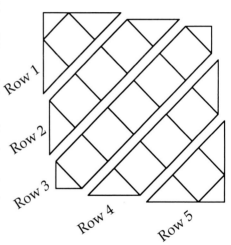

Figure 2

To join borders

1. Join a 5½ x 70½-inch border strip to the left side edge of the quilt top.
2. Repeat with same size strip on the opposite side edge.
3. Join the remaining border strips to the top and bottom edges of the quilt top in the same way.

To prepare for quilting

1. Cut the backing fabric in half crosswise. Then follow the instructions for piecing the backing on page 11.

Figure 3

2. Trace the quilting pattern for the small triangles on page 73. To create the quilting pattern for the large triangles, trace the same pattern, then turn the tracing over and trace again to make a feathered half-circle.

3. Transfer the appropriate quilting pattern to each small and large white triangle (see Figure 3 and page 11).

4. Trace the quilting pattern for the border on page 75 and transfer around the quilt.

5. For added interest you can add a grid (see page 13) over all remaining white areas of the quilt.

To quilt

1. With wrong sides together and batting between, pin the quilt top, batting and backing together.

2. Starting in the center and working outward in a sunburst pattern, take long, loose basting stitches through all 3 layers.

3. Using small running stitches, quilt along all drawn lines. Do not stitch into the seam allowance around the outside edges.

To finish

1. When all quilting is complete remove the basting stitches.

2. Trim batting to ¼ inch smaller than the quilt top all around. Trim backing to same size as quilt top. Turn the raw edges of the backing and quilt top to the wrong side ¼ inch and press. Pin together and machine-stitch or slipstitch all around.

Pillow

Finished Size: 16 x 16 inches

Materials

Note: Yardages are figured for fabric 45 inches wide.

1 yard white fabric
4 x 4-inch square each yellow, lavender and
    pink fabric
small amount of green fabric
thin quilt batting, 17 x 17 inches
2 yards green corded welting
freezer paper
polyester stuffing or 16-inch pillow form

Directions

Follow the quilt directions to prepare the templates and to make 1 appliqué block.

To quilt

1. From the remaining white fabric cut 2 squares, each 17 x 17 inches.
2. Pin the appliqué block to the batting, then to one fabric square. Save the other square for the pillow back.
3. Using small running stitches through all 3 layers of fabric, quilt ¼ inch away from the edges of each appliqué piece.
4. Trim the batting and the fabric square ¼ inch smaller than the pillow top all around. Do not trim the appliquéd block.

To finish

1. With raw edges matching, pin the welting around the front of the pillow top, easing around corners. Using a zipper/cording foot, machine-baste, joining ends of welting neatly.
2. With right sides together and welting between, pin the pillow back to the pillow top, and, using the welting stitches as a guide, stitch around 4 corners and 3 sides.
3. Trim the corners and the seam allowances.
4. Turn right side out and press. Turn the raw edges of the opening to the wrong side ¼ inch and press.
5. Stuff or insert a pillow form and slipstitch opening closed.

Valance

Trace and prepare templates A, B and G as for the quilt top.

Materials

1 x 8-inch pine board for wooden valance, long
   enough to fit window plus returns (see below)
1 package 1½-inch finishing nails
staple gun
white glue (optional)
muslin to fit valance, adding 14 inches to the
   length measurement and 6 inches
   to the width measurement
thin quilt batting same size as muslin
small pieces of pink, yellow, lavender and
   green fabric

Directions

Trace pattern pieces and prepare the templates as for the quilt and pillow projects. Since there are four tulips, use one of the fabric colors twice.

To make wooden valance

1. Measure across the window from the outside edge of each side of the window molding and cut the pine board to this length. Cut 2 pieces, each 6 inches, from the remaining pine board. These are the returns.
2. Nail the returns to each end of the valance to create a U-shape.
3. Wrap the front and sides of the valance with quilt batting and staple to the underside of the board, or glue the batting to the wood.

To appliqué

1. Center the muslin on the front of the valance and mark each corner.
2. Remove the muslin and fold the fabric to make a crease between the top corners and another crease between the bottom corners to mark off the area where you will position the appliqués.
3. Position and pin the flower units so they are evenly spaced across the muslin (see color photograph).
4. Apply to the background as for the quilt and pillow projects.

To finish

1. Position the appliquéd muslin over the padded valance and pull the excess fabric to the underside of the wood while stapling it in position all around.

2. Position the valance over the wood molding at the sides of the window so the top of the molding and the top of the valance are even. Nail the sides of the return (right through the muslin) to each side of the window molding. Pull the muslin away from the nails on each side and the nailhead will disappear behind the fabric.

SPRING TULIPS FOR THE BEDROOM

Feather Quilting Pattern
for Small/Large Triangles

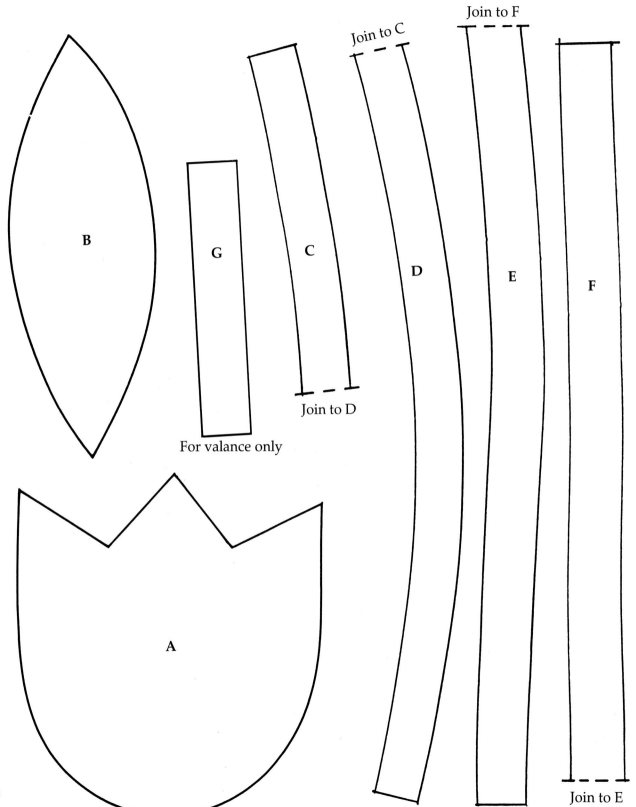

Join to C

Join to F

Join to E

B

G

C

D

E

F

Join to D

For valance only

A

Join to E

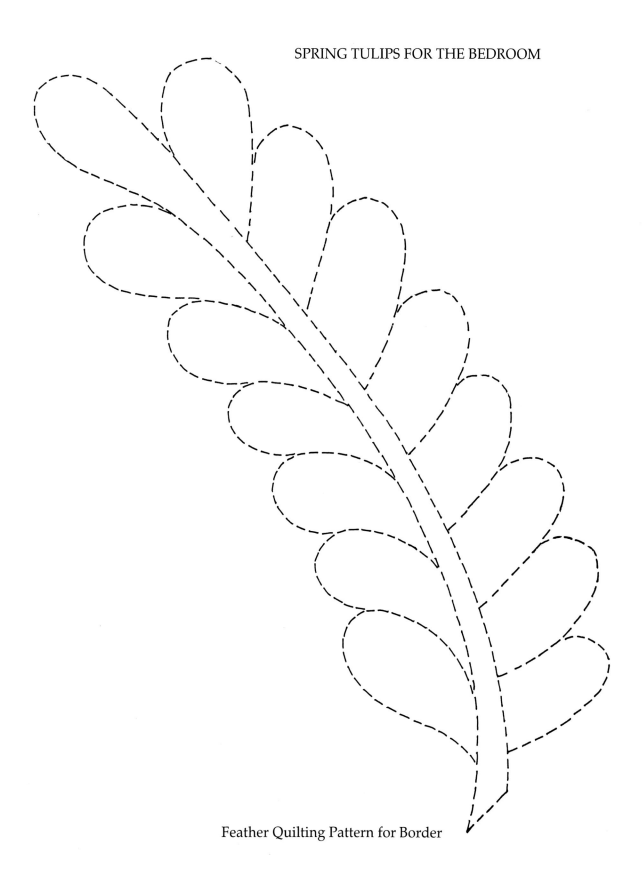

Feather Quilting Pattern for Border

✦ ROMANTIC ✦ PILLOWS

Patricia Loiacono combines all sorts of recycled lace, embroidered doilies, linen tablecloths and napkins, and lovely fabrics to make romantic pillows. Just looking at them piled on a wicker chaise in a sunroom (or on a bed) makes one think of bygone days when the pace was a bit slower. These pillows would make a nice decorating change for summer living. While it may not be possible to duplicate exactly the pillows shown here, they will serve as inspiration for designing your own one-of-a-kind projects. Each is easy to make. The interest comes from the fabrics and trims.

Patchwork Florals

Finished Size: Large pillow 12 x 12 inches; small pillow 5 x 6 inches. However, you can easily alter the sizes to take advantage of scraps of interesting vintage fabrics you may have found.

Materials

large pillow (upper right)
solid brocade, 9½ x 12½ inches
floral fabric, 3½ x 12½-inch strip
backing fabric, 12½ x 12½ inches
polyester stuffing or 12-inch pillow form
small pillow (center left)
pink moiré fabric, 3½ x 6½ inches
floral fabric, 2½ x 6½-inch strip
backing fabric, 5½ x 6½ inches
2-inch piece of lace or eyelet
polyester stuffing

Directions (for both pillows)

Note: All measurements include ¼-inch seam allowance. Join pieces with right sides together, taking ¼-inch seams. Press seams to one side.

1. Join the large solid fabric piece to the floral strip along one long edge.
2. Join the backing to the front around 4 corners and 3 sides, leaving the top of the floral edge open. Trim corners and seam allowances. Turn right side out and press.
3. Turn the raw edges of the opening to the wrong side and press.
4. Stuff pillow to the desired firmness or insert pillow form.
5. For the small pillow only: Insert one edge of the lace in the center of the pillow opening and pin in position.
6. For both pillows: Slipstitch the openings closed.

Embroidered Doily Pillow
(lower right)

Finished Size: 16 x 16 inches

Materials

Note: Yardage is figured for fabric 45 inches wide.

½ yard green moiré fabric (includes backing)
1 embroidered doily or placemat (or use a
    floral fabric)
polyester stuffing or 16-inch pillow form

Directions

To appliqué

Note: All measurements include ¼-inch seam allowance.

1. Cut the corners off a doily or placemat. If using fabric cut a 4-inch square in half on the diagonal to make 2 triangles.
2. Turn the long edge of each triangle under ¼ inch and press.
3. From the moiré fabric, cut 2 squares, each 16½ x 16½ inches.
3. Pin the fabric triangles or doily corners to the top corners of one moiré fabric square.
4. Position the doily or placemat on this moiré square so a band of moiré is visible between the doily and the corners. Trim the bottom edge of the doily if necessary to match the bottom edge of the fabric. Pin in place. (If you are using a piece of floral fabric for the appliqué, cut a curved shape to the desired size, turn the raw edges under ½ inch and press. Pin this shape to the background fabric.) The edge of the doily shown here is finished with embroidery trim and was used as is.
5. Machine-stitch or slipstitch the pressed edges of the corners and the curved edge of the doily to the moiré background.

To finish

Finish as for the large patchwork floral pillow.

Crochet Doily Pillow
(lower left)

Finished Size: 9 x 12 inches

Materials

Note: Yardages are figured for fabric 45 inches wide.

½ yard pink moiré fabric (includes backing)
1 crochet doily
polyester stuffing

Directions

Note: All measurements include ¼-inch seam allowance.

1. Cut the doily in half crosswise. Save one half for another project.
2. Cut 2 pieces of moiré fabric, each 9½ x 12½ inches.
3. Pin the raw edge of the half-doily to the top raw edge of one piece of moiré fabric. Baste in place. Finish as for large floral patchwork pillow.

Floral-Cornered Pillow
(top left)

Finished Size: 16 x 16 inches

Materials

Note: Yardages are figured for fabric 45 inches wide.

½ yard pale green moiré fabric (includes
    backing)
floral fabric, 6 x 6 inch square
polyester stuffing or 16-inch pillow form

Directions

Note: All measurements include ¼-inch seam allowance.

1. Cut the floral fabric square diagonally in both directions to make 4 small triangles.
2. Turn the long edge of each triangle under ¼ inch and press.
3. Cut 2 squares from the moiré fabric, each 16½ x 16½ inches.
4. Position and pin a triangle to each corner of one square of moiré for the pillow top.
5. Machine-stitch or slipstitch the turned edge of each triangle in place.

To finish
Finish as for large floral patchwork pillow.

◆ PASTEL PILLOWS ◆ AND SHAMS

Everyone who sews likes to find projects for using the small scraps left over from larger projects. But making the random scraps work together to create a harmonious finished project requires selectivity.

The newest decorating style is called "formal country." It's a lighter, more streamlined, subtler approach than the earlier, more cluttered style. To achieve this look, use the soft pastels from your scrap basket to make simple pillows and pillow shams. Or, buy a quarter-yard of four to six different fabrics and cut the number of squares needed for each project.

A combination of floral prints and stripes was used for the two matching patchwork pillows, made with two-inch squares. The pillow shams behind them have bands of diamond patchwork down each side, and the white area is quilted in a diamond grid pattern. The little fence rail pillow in the front was made with fabrics from the 1920s and blends well with the fabrics used for the other projects.

Patch Pillows

Finished Size: 18 x 18 inches

These pillows are generously sized for use as a back rest on a bed. The simple patchwork pattern is a version of the nine-patch pattern, so called because it is created from nine blocks of nine squares each. These pillows are not quilted; however, if you'd like to add hand quilting, add ½ yard each of quilt batting and muslin (enough for two pillows) to the materials list.

Materials

Note: Yardages are figured for fabric 45 inches wide.

a variety of fabric scraps to make 81 squares
    using pattern A (162 squares for 2 pillows)
⅝ yard of muslin or pale fabric for backing
    (1¼ yards for 2 pillows)
polyester stuffing or 18-inch pillow form
tracing paper
cardboard

Directions

Note: All measurements and patterns include ¼-inch seam allowance. Join pieces with right sides together, taking ¼-inch seams. Press seams open.

Trace pattern A on page 87 and transfer to cardboard to make a template (see page 11).

Cut the following:

from print scraps:
    81 A

from muslin or backing fabric:
    1 piece, 18½ x 18½ inches

To make a block

1. Begin by arranging 9 squares in a pleasing pattern of 3 squares by 3 rows. Rearrange the squares until you find the most appealing arrangement.

2. Join the first square in row 1 to the next square along one side edge. Repeat with the last square in row 1.
3. Make 3 rows in this way.
4. Make 9 blocks of 9 squares each.

To make a row

1. Lay out the blocks in a pleasing arrangement of 3 rows of 3 blocks each.
2. With seams aligned, join all 3 blocks in row 1 along one side edge.
3. Repeat with rows 2 and 3.

To join rows

1. With seams aligned, join the bottom edge of row 1 to the top edge of row 2.
2. Join the bottom edge of row 2 to the top edge of row 3 in the same way.

To quilt (optional)

1. Cut a piece of muslin or other fabric the same size as the patchwork piece.
2. Cut a piece of thin quilt batting the same size as the patchwork piece.
3. With batting between, pin the patchwork top and muslin together.
4. Take small running stitches (see page 9) through all layers ¼ inch away from each side of all seamlines. Remove pins. Trim batting and muslin to ¼ inch smaller than patchwork top all around.

To finish

1. With right sides together, pin pillow back and patchwork top together.
2. Stitch around 4 corners and 3 sides, leaving one side open for turning.
3. Trim corners and seam allowances.
4. Turn right side out and press.
5. Turn raw edges ¼ inch to the wrong side and press.
6. Stuff or insert pillow form and slipstitch opening closed.

Quilted Sham

Finished Size: 22½ x 33½ inches (to hold standard-size bed pillow)

Materials (for one sham)

Note: Yardages are figured for fabric 45 inches wide.

2¼ yards muslin
a variety of pastel print fabric scraps
¾ yard thin quilt batting
polyester stuffing
tracing paper
cardboard
marking pencil
ruler

Directions

Note: All measurements and patterns include ¼-inch seam allowance. Join pieces with right sides together, taking ¼-inch seams. Press seams open unless instructed otherwise.

Trace patterns A, B and C on page 87 and transfer to cardboard for templates (see page 11).

Cut the following:

from a variety of pastel print scraps:
   46 A

from muslin:
   32 B
   8 C
   1 piece 15 x 23 inches
   2 pieces, each 4½ x 23 inches
   2 pieces, each 23 x 34½ inches (1 for backing)

from batting:
   1 piece, 22½ x 33½ inches

To make patchwork bands

1. Refer to Figure 1. For row 1, join one side edge of a B piece to the left side edge of an A piece.
2. Join another B piece to the right side edge of the A piece as shown.
3. Join the diagonal edge of a C piece to the top edge of the A piece as shown.
4. Repeat for row 9.

To make rows

1. Refer to Figure 2. For row 2, join the diagonal edge of a C piece to the left side edge of an A piece, followed by another A piece, then another A piece, and end with a B piece. Repeat for row 8.
2. Join a B piece to an A piece, followed by 2 more A pieces, and end with a B piece. Make a total of 5 for rows 3 through 7.

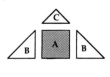

Figure 1

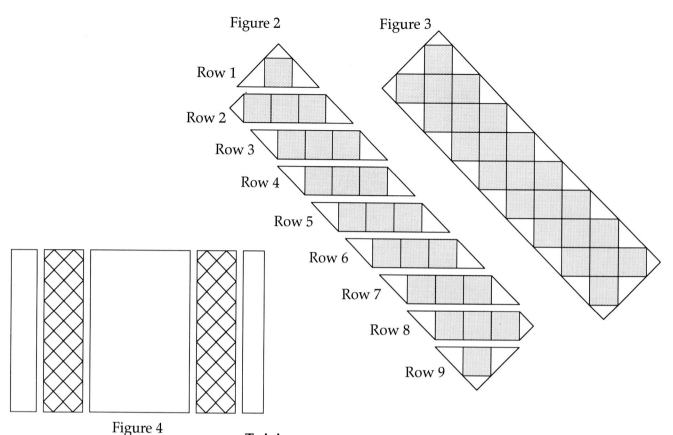

Figure 2   Figure 3

Row 1
Row 2
Row 3
Row 4
Row 5
Row 6
Row 7
Row 8
Row 9

Figure 4

To join rows

1. Refer to Figure 3. Join the bottom edge of row 1 to the top edge of row 2.

2. Continue to join remaining rows in this way. Make another patchwork band in this way.

To make pillow sham top

1. Refer to Figure 4. Join a 4½ x 23-inch muslin strip along the left side edge of one patchwork band. Press seams to the patchwork side.

2. Next, join the 15 x 23-inch muslin piece to the other long edge of the patchwork band, followed by the second patchwork band, and end with the remaining muslin strip to complete the top.

To quilt

1. Using the seamlines of the patchwork bands as a guide, draw a grid of quilting lines over the muslin fabric with marker and ruler.

2. With wrong sides together and batting between, pin the patchwork top, batting, and one of the remaining muslin pieces together.

3. Take small running stitches (see page 9) along all drawn lines. If desired, take small running stitches ¼ inch away from each side of all seamlines. Do not run stitches into the seam allowance around the outside edges.

To finish

1. Remove all pins.
2. Join the backing fabric to the quilted patchwork top along one short end and along both long edges.
3. Trim corners and seam allowances. Turn right side out and press.
4. Turn the raw edges of the remaining end ¼ inch to the wrong side and press.
5. Turn under another ¼ inch and press. Stuff or insert pillow and machine-stitch or slipstitch all around.

Fence Rail Pillow

You can use random fabric colors and prints to make this project or, for a more traditional rendering of this design, combine light, medium and dark colors to make each block.

Finished Size: 9 x 12 inches

Materials

a variety of fabric scraps to make 36 pieces
    from pattern D
⅜ yard muslin (or one of the patchwork
    fabrics) for backing
polyester stuffing
tracing paper
cardboard

Directions

Note: All measurements and the pattern include ¼-inch seam allowance. Join pieces with right sides together, taking ¼-inch seams. Press seams open.

    Trace pattern D and transfer to cardboard to make a template (see page 11).

Cut the following:
from print scraps:
    36 D
from muslin:
    1 piece, 9½ x 12½ inches (for backing)

To make a block

1. Refer to Figure 5. Join 2 different D pieces along one long edge.

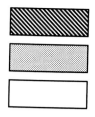

Figure 5

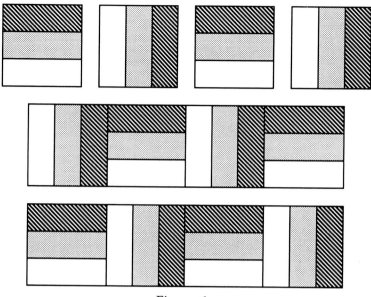

Figure 6

2. Join another D piece in the same way, as shown. Make 12 blocks in this way.

To make rows

1. Refer to Figure 6. Arrange all the blocks as shown before joining them.
2. Join the first block in row 1 to the second block along one edge.
3. Continue to join 2 more blocks in this way to complete row 1.
4. Following the layout in Figure 6 make 2 more rows of 4 blocks each.

To join rows

1. With seams aligned, join the bottom edge of row 1 to the top edge of row 2 (see Figure 6).
2. Next, with seams aligned, join the bottom edge of row 2 to the top edge of row 3 in the same way to complete the pillow top.

To finish

Note: If you'd like to quilt this pillow top, refer to the directions for quilting the patch pillows on page 82. Then proceed as follows:

1. Pin the patchwork pillow top to the muslin backing piece.
2. Stitch around 4 corners and 3 sides, leaving an opening for turning.
3. Trim corners and seam allowances.
4. Turn right side out and press.
5. Turn the raw edges ¼ inch to the wrong side and press.
6. Stuff and slipstitch the opening closed.

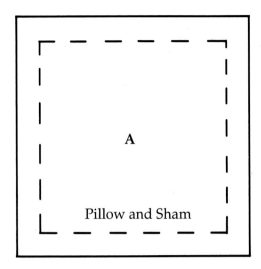

A

Pillow and Sham

Sham

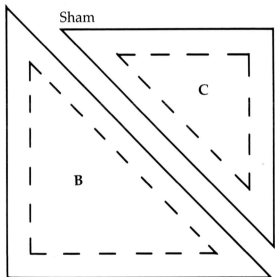

B

C

Fence Rail

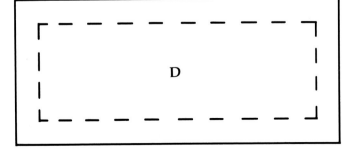

D

YANKEE STAR SHOWER CURTAIN

A patchwork shower curtain is an unusual project that can add a unique decorating touch to the bathroom. The grommets and attaching tool come in a package available at home centers, notions department, and dime stores. However, you can substitute buttonholes for hanging if you prefer. The Yankee Star pattern is an old New England design that fits in perfectly with this early 1800s house on Nantucket Island. This project can be adapted for use as a bed cover as well.

Finished Size: 70 x 74 inches

Materials

Note: Yardages are figured for fabric 45 inches wide.

a variety of assorted pastel prints totaling
    3½ yards
1⅛ yards peach calico (border D pieces)
⅝ yard blue calico (border E pieces)
2¼ yards blue striped fabric (top and bottom
    borders)
4¼ yards of backing fabric
12 grommets and grommet attaching tool
tracing paper
cardboard

Cutting List

Note: All measurements include ¼-inch seam allowance. Join all pieces with right sides together, taking ¼-inch seams. Press seams to one side.

    Trace patterns A, B, C, D and E on pages 92-94 and transfer to cardboard for templates (see page 11).

Cut the following:
from assorted prints:
    80 A (use 8 for pieced borders)
    72 B (cut 36 in reverse)
    36 C
    9 squares, each 6½ x 6½ inches

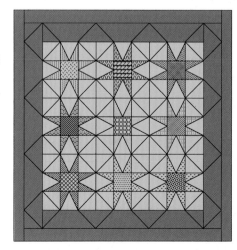

Figure 1a

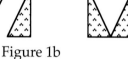

Figure 1b

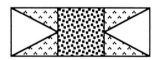

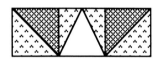

Figure 2a

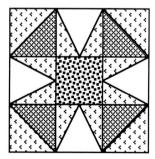

Figure 2b

from peach calico:
  12 D

from blue calico:
  12 E

from blue stripe:
  2 strips, each 4½ x 66½ inches (for top and bottom outer borders)
  2 strips, each 2½ x 74½ inches (for side outer borders)

Directions

To make a block

1. Refer to Figure 1a. Join 2 different A pieces along the diagonal to make a square as shown. Make 4 squares in this way.
2. Refer to Figure 1b. Join one diagonal edge of a B piece to one diagonal edge of a C piece of a different fabric. Then join another B piece of the same fabric as the first B piece (cut in reverse), to the other diagonal edge of the C piece to make a square as shown. Make 4 squares in this way.
3. Refer to Figure 2a. Join a square made in step 1 to a square made in step 2 along one side edge as shown. Then join another step 1 square to complete the top row of the block. Repeat step 3 to make the bottom row of the block.
4. Refer to Figure 2a. To make the middle row of the block, join 2 squares made in step 2 to a 6½ x 6½ inch square. Note that the pieced squares have been turned 90 degrees.
5. Refer to Figure 2b. With seams aligned, stitch the bottom edge of the top row to the top edge of the middle row. Then stitch the bottom edge of the middle row to the top edge of the bottom row to complete the block. Make 9 blocks in this way.

To make rows

With seams aligned, join 3 blocks to make a row. Make 3 rows of 3 blocks each.

To join rows

With seams aligned, join the bottom edge of the first row to the top edge of the second row. Then join the bottom edge of the second row to the top edge of the third row in the same way.

To make pieced borders

1. Refer to Figure 3a. Join the diagonal edge of an A piece to a diagonal edge of a peach calico D piece. Then join one diagonal edge of a blue calico E piece to the other diagonal edge of the D piece.
2. Continue with another D piece, then an E piece, another D piece, and end with another A piece. Make 2 strips in this way for the top and bottom pieced borders.

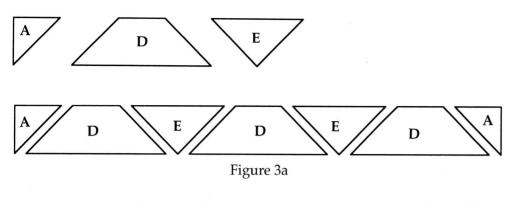

Figure 3a

Figure 3b

3. Refer to Figure 3b. Join the diagonal edge of an A piece to one diagonal edge of a blue E piece. Then join a peach D piece to the other side edge of the E piece.

4. Continue with another E piece, then a D piece, another E piece, a D piece, another E piece, and end the strip with another A piece as shown. Make 2 strips in this way for the side pieced borders.

To join borders

Refer to Figure 4.

1. Join one of the shorter pieced border strips to the top edge of the shower curtain.

2. Next, join the other short border strip to the bottom edge of the shower curtain as shown.

3. Join the remaining pieced border strips to the side edges of the shower curtain.

4. Join one of the shorter blue striped outer border strips to the top edge of the shower curtain. Repeat on the bottom edge.

5. Join the remaining blue striped outer border strips to the side edges of the shower curtain.

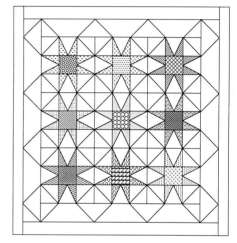

Figure 4

To finish

1. Cut the backing fabric in half crosswise. Then follow the instructions for piecing the backing on page 11.

2. With right sides together, center the pieced shower curtain over the backing. Trim the backing to the same size as the shower curtain. Pin edges together.

3. Stitch around 3 sides and 4 corners, leaving an opening along top edge for turning. Trim corners and turn right side out. Press. Pin opening edges together and machine-stitch or slipstitch closed.

4. For grommet placement, measure down 2 inches from the top of the blue striped border. Then measure in 1 inch from each side edge of the

top border and make a pencil mark. Make 10 more marks evenly spaced between the end marks for a total of 12. Apply grommets, following manufacturer's instructions. If you are making buttonholes instead of using grommets, measure and mark in the same way. For a bed cover, omit grommets.

YANKEE STAR SHOWER CURTAIN PATTERNS

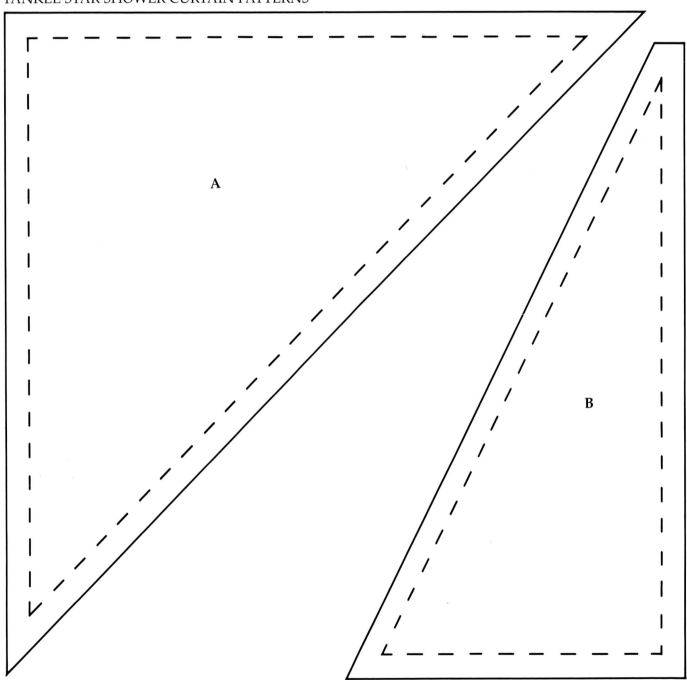

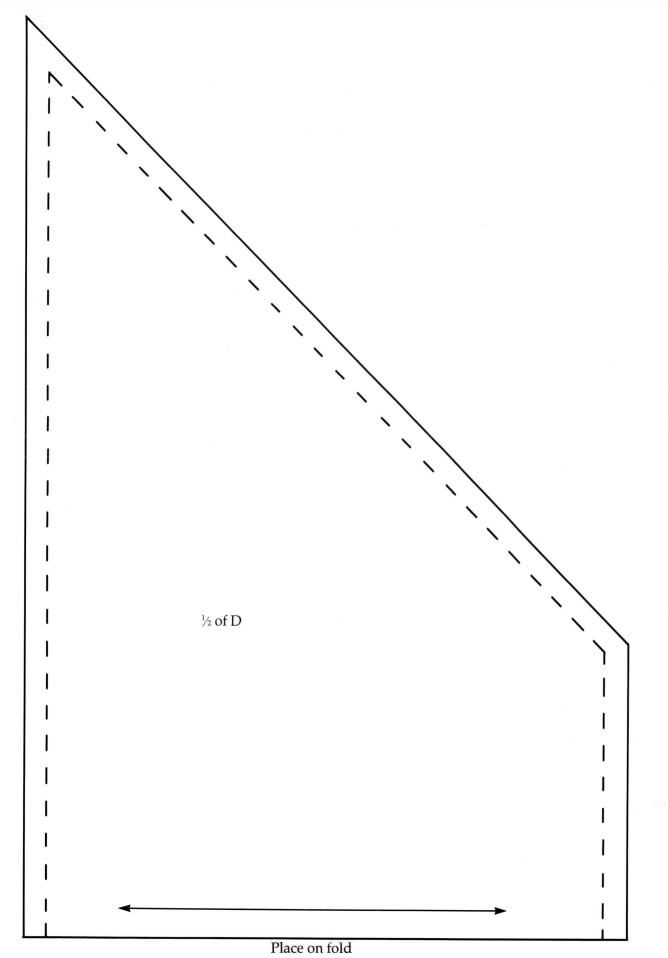

½ of D

Place on fold

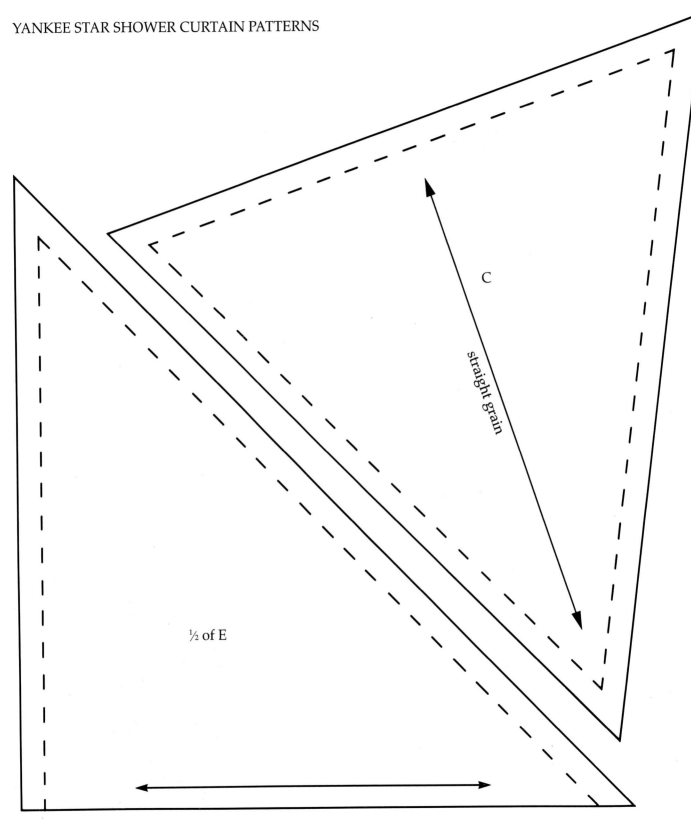

C

straight grain

½ of E

Place on fold

✦ FESTIVE TABLE ✦ COVER

This lively patchwork table cover can also double as a bed quilt (it will fit a single bed) or as a throw. This quilt would also look nice if made with a combination of calico prints and solid colors. The checkerboard blocks are made with the strip piecing method, a quick-and-easy way to piece small squares of fabric.

Finished Size: 74 x 74 inches

Materials

Note: Yardages are figured for fabric 45 inches wide.

1 yard pink fabric
1½ yards green fabric
2 yards brick red fabric
5⅜ yards blue fabric (includes backing fabric)
2½ yards unbleached muslin
quilt batting, 74 x 74 inches
tracing paper
cardboard

Note: All measurements include ¼-inch seam allowance. Join all pieces with right sides together, taking ¼-inch seams. Press seams to one side or to the darker side.

Trace patterns A and B and transfer them to cardboard for templates (see page 11).

Cutting list

Cut the following:

from pink:
   14 strips, each 2½ x 45 inches

from green:
   100 A

from brick red:
   2 strips, each 2½ x 62½ inches (for top and bottom inner borders)
   2 strips, each 2½ x 66½ inches (for side inner borders)

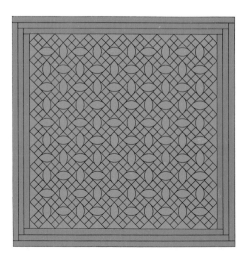

from blue:

    14 strips, each 2½ x 45 inches

    2 strips, each 2½ x 70½ inches (for top and bottom outer borders)

    2 strips, each 2½ x 74½ inches (for side outer borders)

    Save remaining fabric for backing (see **"To finish,"** step 1, page 99)

from muslin:

    2 strips, each 2½x 66½ inches (for top and bottom middle borders)

    2 strips, each 2½ x 70½ inches (for side middle borders)

    200 B

    20 squares, each 4⅞ x 4⅞ inches; cut each square diagonally into 2 triangles each.

    2 squares, each 3¾ x 3¾ inches; cut each square diagonally into 2 triangles each.

Directions

To make block 1

Refer to strip piecing, page 14.

1. Stitch one long edge of a 2½ x 45-inch blue strip to one long edge of the same size pink strip.

2. Repeat with the remaining blue and pink strips to make 14 sets of blue and pink strips.

3. Measure and mark across each set of strips in 2½ inch segments (18 segments per set). You will have a total of 252 segments of which you will use only 242.

4. Refer to Figure 1. Join two segments along one side edge, alternating blue and pink, to make a block as shown.

5. Make 121 blocks in this way.

To make block 2

Refer to page 12 for joining curved edges.

1. Join a curved edge of a green A piece to a curved edge of a muslin B piece. Clip into the seam allowance at regular intervals, then press seams to the green side.

2. Repeat with another muslin B piece on the opposite curved edge of the green A piece to complete the block as shown in Figure 2.

3. Make 100 blocks in this way.

To make rows

1. Refer to Figure 3a. For row 1, join a short edge of a large muslin triangle to the left side edge of a pieced checkerboard block 1.

2. Next, stitch the short edge of another large muslin triangle to the right side edge of this pieced block.

3. Stitch the diagonal edge of a small muslin triangle across the top edge of the pieced block as shown to complete row 1.

Figure 1   Figure 2

Figure 3a

Figure 3b

Figure 3c

97

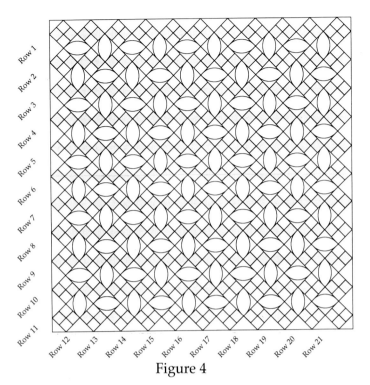

Row 1
Row 2
Row 3
Row 4
Row 5
Row 6
Row 7
Row 8
Row 9
Row 10
Row 11
Row 12
Row 13
Row 14
Row 15
Row 16
Row 17
Row 18
Row 19
Row 20
Row 21

Figure 4

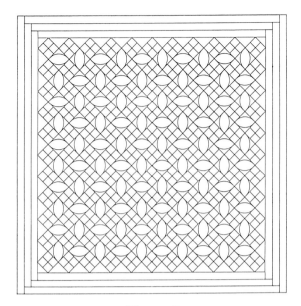

Figure 5

4. Refer to Figure 3b. To make row 2, join the short edge of a large muslin triangle to another pieced block 1, followed by a block 2, another block 1, then another large muslin triangle, to complete the row.

5. Refer to Figures 3c and 4 and continue to make all 21 rows in the lengths required.

To join rows

Refer to Figure 4 for setting rows.

1. With seams aligned, stitch the bottom edge of row 1 to the top edge of row 2.

2. Next, stitch the bottom edge of row 2 to the top edge of row 3.

3. Continue to join all 21 rows in this way to make the patchwork top.

To join borders

Refer to Figure 5 and color photograph.

1. Stitch one of the short red strips to the top edge of the patchwork top. Repeat on the bottom edge.

2. Next, stitch the remaining red border strips to the side edges.

3. Stitch one of the short muslin border strips to the top edge of the patchwork top. Repeat on the bottom edge.

4. Next, stitch the remaining muslin border strips to the side edges of the patchwork top.

5. Stitch one of the short blue border strips to the top edge. Repeat on the bottom edge.

6. Next, join the remaining blue border strips to the side edges.

To finish

Since this patchwork project is used as a table cover no quilting is necessary. However, if you want to add hand-quilting stitches, refer to page 13 for details on how to quilt.

1. For backing, use the blue fabric you saved after cutting the small strips and border strips. You should have enough to cut one 74½-inch length across the full width of the fabric, plus an equal length about 35 inches wide, left after cutting the border strips. Follow the instructions for piecing the backing on page 11, using the 35-inch wide piece as the center panel.

2. With wrong sides together and batting between, pin the quilt top, batting and backing together.

3. Trim the backing and batting ½ inch smaller than the quilt top all around.

4. Turn the raw edges of the patchwork top under ¼ inch all around and press. Then turn the edges of the top ¼ inch over the backing all around to make a binding.

5. Machine-stitch or slipstitch the turned edges in place all around. Remove all pins.

FESTIVE TABLE COVER PATTERNS

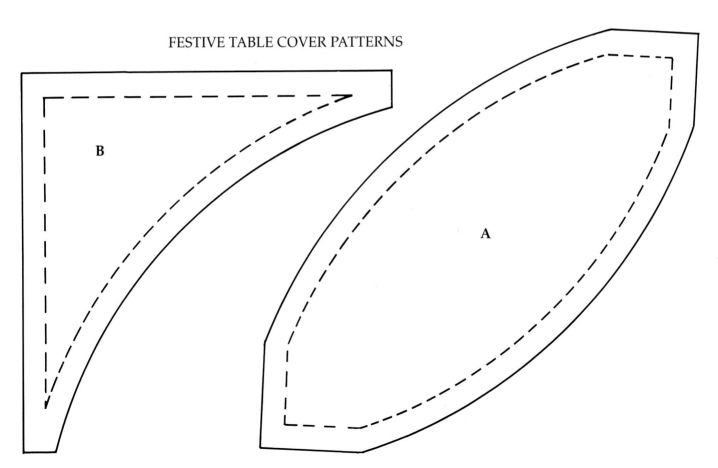

✦ SENSATIONAL ✦ SACHETS

Old lace, vintage fabrics and pieces from old clothing are the materials Patricia Loiacono uses to make sachets, pin cushions and pillows for Ophelia's, her Medford, Massachusetts, shop. Look in flea markets and second-hand stores for old linen, ribbons, buttons and fabric from bedspreads or draperies. Recycled materials such as these are very popular in the 90s. Suggested fabrics: satin, tapestry, linen, moiré or velvet. You might want to make several sachets for gift giving or to sell at craft fairs. These two sachets would also make nice cushions for holding decorative pins.

Finished Size: 5 x 6 inches each

Materials

scraps of solid and printed fabrics
backing fabric 5½ x 6½ inches for each sachet
12 inches ribbon or seam binding to match a
    color in the fabrics
scrap of lace
stuffing
small amount potpourri
tracing paper

Directions

Note: All templates and measurements include ¼-inch seam allowance. Join all pieces with right sides together, taking ¼-inch seams. Press seams open.

Sachet 1 (left)

Trace templates and cut out to use as patterns.

Cut the following:

from print:
    1 A
from solid:
    1 A

To assemble

1. Join the print and solid pieces along one long edge.
2. Stitch the backing and front pieces together, leaving a 3-inch opening across the top edge.

To finish

1. Turn right side out and press.
2. Fill with a combination of stuffing and potpourri to give the sachet softness and a bit of scent.
3. Turn the opening edges ¼ inch to the wrong side and pin closed.
4. Using a zipper/cording foot, and with the front facing up, machine-stitch all around ⅛ inch from the edge.
5. Tack a bit of lace and a ribbon to the center of the top edge.

Sachet 2 (right)

Cut the following:

from solid:
    1 B

from print:
    1 C

To assemble

1. Join the solid and print pieces as shown in the color photograph.
2. Continue to assemble and finish the sachet as for Sachet 1.

SENSATIONAL SACHETS PATTERNS

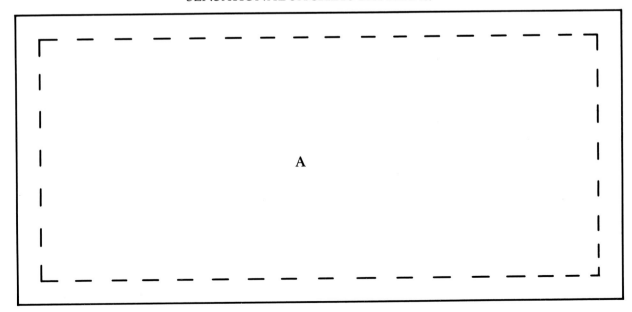

A

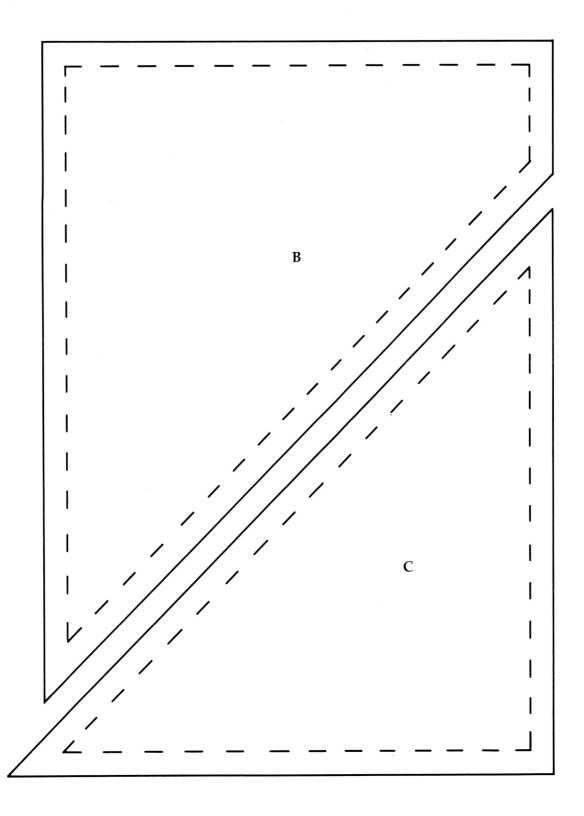

B

C

◆ PINWHEEL ◆ WALL QUILT

This colorful wall quilt is fun to make. It's easy to piece the pinwheel blocks, and no hand quilting is required. Made with soft baby prints and colors, this pattern becomes a cradle quilt.

Finished Size: 29½ x 37 inches

Materials

Note: Yardages are figured for fabric 45 inches wide.

½ yard bright print fabric
½ yard dark blue fabric
½ yard yellow fabric
¼ yard teal fabric
¼ yard purple fabric
1⅛ yards backing fabric
1 yard thin quilt batting
tracing paper
cardboard

Note: All measurements and the template include ¼-inch seam allowance. Join all pieces with right sides together, taking ¼-inch seams. Press seams to one side unless instructed otherwise.

Trace pattern on page 108 and transfer to cardboard for templates (see page 11).

Directions

Cut the following:

from bright print:
    48 from template

from dark blue:
    48 from template

from yellow:
    9 strips, each 2 x 6½ inches
    2 strips, each 2 x 21½ inches
    2 strips, each 2 x 29 inches
    2 strips, each 2 x 32 inches

from teal:
    2 strips, each 2 x 24½ inches (for top and bottom borders)
    2 strips, each 2 x 35 inches (for side borders)

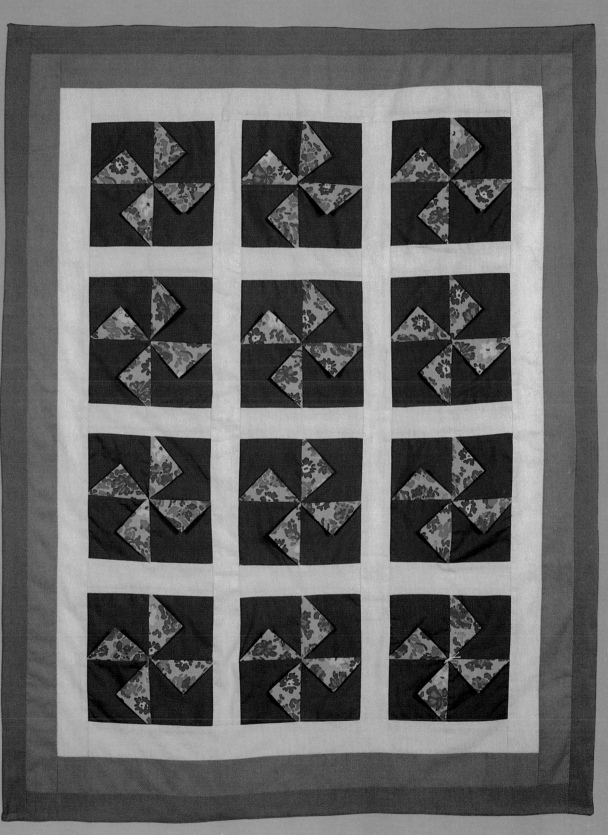

from purple:
      2 strips, each 2 x 27½ inches (for top and bottom borders)
      2 strips, each 2 x 37½ inches (for side borders)

Directions

To make pinwheel blocks

1. Refer to Figure 1a. With wrong sides together, fold the print pieces in half diagonally and press. Fold in half again into a smaller triangle. All the raw edges should line up evenly. The triangles will have one side with a double folded edge and one side with 2 single folded edges. These edges will be referred to for correct placement on the background squares.

2. With right sides up and raw edges aligned, pin one triangle to one side edge of a dark blue square as shown in Figure 1b. Make 4 in this way.

3. Refer to Figure 1c and pin a second triangle next to the first triangle so the double folded edges fit tightly together.

4. Refer to Figure 1d. Pin another dark blue square over the pinned triangle section and stitch along one side edge only, as shown. Press seam open and press the second triangle toward the second square as shown in Figure 1e. Repeat with the remaining dark blue squares and print triangles, making a total of 24 sets of two squares.

5. Refer to Figure 1f for placement. With right sides together and 4 triangle points in the center, pin 2 sets together and stitch along one long edge. Press seam open.

6. Make 12 blocks in this way.

To make rows

1. Refer to Figure 2. With right sides together, join one short yellow strip to the bottom edge of a block.

2. Next, join the top edge of another block to the bottom edge of the yellow strip in the same way.

3. Continue with another yellow strip, then another block followed by a yellow strip, and end with another block, to make a row of 4 blocks separated by 3 yellow strips as shown. Make 3 rows in this way.

To join rows

1. Refer to Figure 3. Join a 2 x 29-inch yellow strip to the right side edge of row 1. Next, join row 2, followed by another yellow strip, followed by row 3.

2. With right sides together, join the bottom edge of a 2 x 21½-inch yellow strip to the top edge of the pieced blocks. Repeat on the bottom edge of the pieced blocks.

3. Join one of the remaining long yellow strips to the left side edge of the quilt top. Repeat on the right side edge.

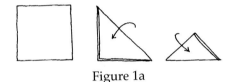

Figure 1a

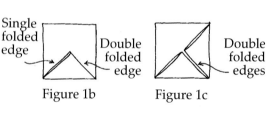

Single folded edge   Double folded edge

Figure 1b   Figure 1c   Double folded edges

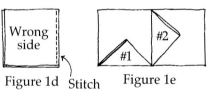

Wrong side

Figure 1d   Stitch   Figure 1e

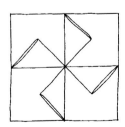

Figure 1f

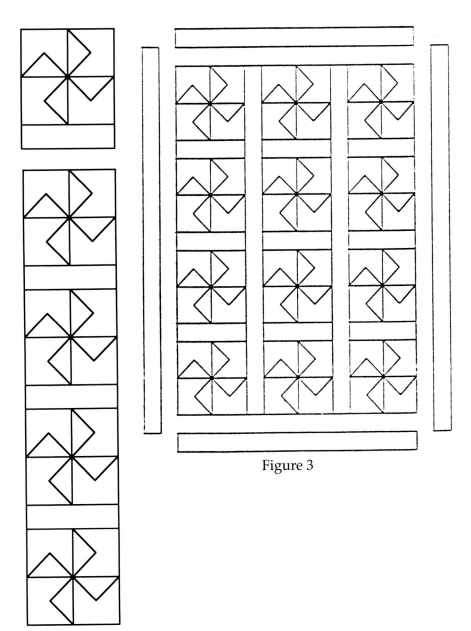

Figure 2

Figure 3

Figure 4

To join borders

1. Refer to Figure 4. Join one of the short teal border strips to the top edge of the quilt top. Repeat across the bottom edge.

2. Join one of the remaining teal border strips to one side edge of the quilt top. Repeat on the other side edge.

3. Join one of the short purple border strips to the top edge of the quilt top. Repeat on the bottom edge.

4. Next, join the remaining purple border strips to each side edge of the quilt top.

To finish

1. Place the batting on the wrong side of the backing fabric. Then, with right side up, center the patchwork top over the batting.
2. Pin all 3 layers together.
3. Trim the batting and backing fabric ½ inch smaller than the quilt top all around.
4. Turn the raw edges of the top under ¼ inch and press. Then turn the edges over onto the backing ¼ inch all around.
5. Slipstitch the turned edges in place.

To hang

See page 15.

PINWHEEL WALL QUILT PATTERN

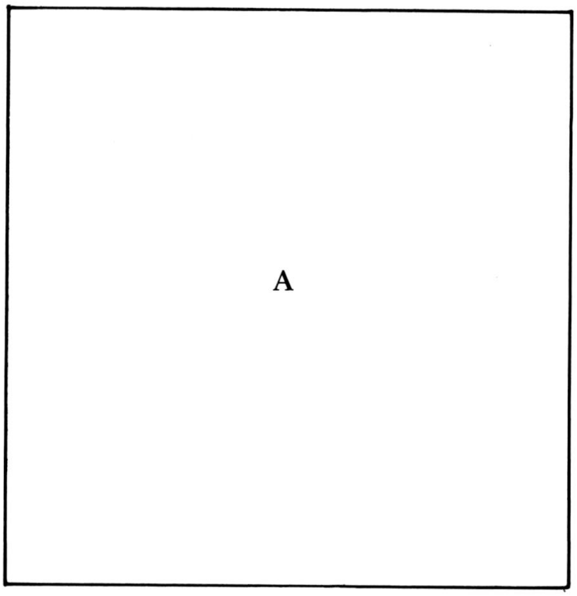

A

PRETTY PERSONALS

The Spring Tulips quilt on page 67 inspired the design of these personal items: a lingerie travel case, a cosmetics pouch and an eyeglass case. When I couldn't find the variety of soft pastel colors I wanted for these projects I used fabric dye to create the exact shades needed. It was quite easy to do and I realized this is a good way to make a quilt from dark and light shades of the same colors.

If you can't find colors to your liking simply buy small amounts of white cotton and fabric dye, and follow the directions on the package.

Finished Sizes: Lingerie case 8 x 13 inches
Cosmetics pouch 3½ x 6½ inches
Eyeglass case 4½ x 8 inches

Note: If using a machine zigzag stitch to apply, cut all appliqué pieces same size as template. If doing hand-sewn appliqué, add ¼-inch seam allowance all around when cutting the appliqué pieces. Measurements for all other construction pieces include ¼-inch seam allowance. Join pieces with right sides together, taking ¼-inch seams.

Lingerie Case

Materials

solid lavender fabric, 8½ x 26½ inches

thin quilt batting, 8½ x 26½ inches

floral print fabric for lining, 9½ x 26½ inches

2 strips floral print fabric, each 1½ x 9 inches
(for optional side trim)

blue, pink and yellow fabric, 5 x 5 inch piece
of each

small piece of green fabric for stems and
leaves

2 small Velcro® tabs, or button or snap for
closure

freezer paper

Directions

To make appliqués

1. Trace patterns A, B, C and D on page 114 onto freezer paper and cut out. Follow the instructions for freezer paper templates on page 12 to prepare the following pieces: 1 each blue, pink and yellow tulip; 2 green leaves; 1 green stem C; 2 green stems D (1 in reverse).

To position appliqués

1. Fold the lavender fabric in half crosswise and press to make a crease on the bottom edge.
2. Open flat and, with right side up, pin to the batting along the side edges.
3. Next, center and position the tulip heads, stems and leaves on the front of the case. Pin in place.

To quilt

1. Use an overcast stitch or slipstitch (page 9) around all appliqué edges through both the background fabric and the batting.
2. If you add more quilting to this project it will have more character. Take small running stitches (page 9) through the fabric and batting ¼ inch away from outside edges of all appliqué pieces and ¼ inch inside the edges of all tulip heads.

To assemble

1. With right sides together, fold the appliquéd fabric in half crosswise.
2. Stitch along the side edges.
3. Turn right side out and press.
4. With right sides together, fold the lining fabric in half crosswise and stitch along the side edges. Do not turn right side out.
5. Insert the lining inside the appliquéd case. There will be extra lining fabric at the top edge all around.
6. Turn the raw top edge to the outside ¼ inch and press.
7. Fold the remaining top fabric to the outside over the top edge of the case and press. Pin in place and slipstitch all around.

To finish

The trim is optional and can be added in the following way:
1. Turn the ends of each floral strip under ¼ inch and press. Then, fold the long raw edges of the strips under ¼ inch and press.
2. Use these strips to encase the side edges so there is ½ inch of fabric on the front and back of the case. Pin in place, then slipstitch the edges to the sides of the case.
3. Attach a small tab of Velcro® inside the front and back of the case, or use a decorative button or snap.

Cosmetics Pouch

Materials

blue fabric, 4 x 13 inches
floral fabric, 4 x 13 inches
thin quilt batting, 4 x 13 inches
small piece each of pink and green fabrics for
     flower, leaf and stem
green and pink thread to match fabric
14 inches of cord for drawstring

Directions

To make appliqués

1. Trace patterns E, G and H and cut out to use as patterns. Do not add seam allowances. Cut 1 pink tulip, 1 green stem G, and 1 green leaf H.

To appliqué

1. With wrong sides together, fold the blue fabric in half crosswise and press to make a crease on the fold. Open fabric flat and, with right side up, pin to the batting.
2. Begin ½ inch down from the top raw edge and center the pink tulip head on the blue fabric. Pin in position.
3. Next, position the green stem so the top edge is slightly under the center of the bottom of the tulip. Pin in place.
4. Pin the leaf in place so the straight edge is tucked under the side edge of the stem.
5. Using a narrow zigzag stitch and thread to match each fabric piece, stitch around all raw edges.

To finish

1. With right sides together, fold the fabric in half on the crease and pin along sides.
2. Beginning ½ inch down from the top, stitch along the side edges. The ½-inch opening is for inserting the cord.
3. Turn right side out and press.
4. With right sides together, fold the lining fabric in half crosswise and stitch along the sides edges. Do not turn right side out.
5. Insert the lining fabric inside the appliquéd pouch.
6. Zigzag-stitch the top edges of the outer fabric and lining together. Then fold the zigzagged edges to the inside of the pouch and press. Pin in place.
7. Measure down ½ inch from the top edge and hand-sew around the

inside of the pouch through the lining and batting but not the outer fabric. This will create a channel for the drawstring.

8. Attach a safety pin to one end of the cord and draw through the side-seam opening. Knot the ends of the cord.

Eyeglass Case

Materials

light purple fabric, 5 x 16½ inches
floral print fabric, 5 x 17½ inches
2 strips floral print fabric, each 1½ x 8½ inches
aqua fabric, 4 x 4 inches
small piece of green fabric for stem and leaves
thin quilt batting, 5 x 16½ inches

Directions

To make appliqués

1. Trace and cut out patterns E, F, G and H. Do not add seam allowances. Cut 1 aqua tulip and 1 each green stem G, leaf F, and leaf H.

To appliqué

1. Fold the light purple fabric in half crosswise and press.
2. Open the fabric and, with right side up, pin to batting along sides.
3. Center the appliqué pieces on the top half of the fabric and pin in place as you did for the Cosmetics Pouch.
4. Using matching thread, zigzag-stitch around all raw edges of each appliqué piece.

To assemble

1. With right sides together, fold the appliquéd fabric in half crosswise and pin sides together.
2. Stitch along the side edges.
3. With right sides together, fold the floral fabric in half crosswise and stitch along the side edges. Do not turn right side out.
4. Insert the lining into the appliquéd case. There will be extra fabric at the top edge.
5. Finish the top edge of the case as you did for the Lingerie Case.

To finish

1. Encase the side edges with the floral strips as you did for the Lingerie Case. Pin in place.
2. Instead of slipstitching, zigzag-stitch the edges in place.

♦ FEATHERED STAR ♦
PILLOW

S tar patterns and their many variations have always been among the most popular designs for quilting projects. This traditional motif is enhanced by the use of a rose on white print combined with a white on red print, all on a white background. Created with red, green and white fabrics instead, this would make a lovely Christmas design.

Finished Size: 18 x 18 inches

Materials

Note: Yardages are figured for fabric 45 inches wide.

⅝ yard white on red print fabric
¼ yard rose on white print fabric
¾ yard solid white fabric (includes backing)
thin quilt batting, 18 x 18 inches
18-inch pillow form or polyester stuffing
tracing paper
cardboard

Cutting List

Note: All measurements and patterns include ¼-inch seam allowance. Join all pieces with right sides together, taking ¼-inch seams. Press seams to one side (the darker side, where applicable).

Trace patterns A, B, C, D, E, F, G and H on page 118, and transfer to cardboard for templates (see page 11).

Cut the following:

from white on red print:
2 strips, each 2½ x 14½ inches (for top and bottom borders)
2 strips, each 2½ x 18½ inches (for side borders)
8 A
8 B
8 D
32 E
8 F

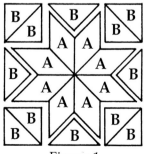

Figure 1

from rose on white print:
 8 B
 8 C
 48 E

from white:
 2 squares, each 18½ x 18½ inches
 4 G
 4 H

Directions

To assemble patchwork

1. Refer to Figure 1. Stitch the 8 white on red A pieces together to make a star as shown.

2. Stitch the diagonal edge of a white on red B piece to the diagonal edge of a rose on white B piece to make a square. Make 4 squares in this way.

3. Join one of these squares into each corner (see page 12 for stitching corners). Then join a rose on white B triangle to each remaining angle between the A pieces to complete the center block as shown.

4. Refer to Figure 2. Stitch one short diagonal edge of a rose on white C piece to each short edge of a white on red B triangle to make the unit as shown. Make 4 in this way.

5. Stitch one of these units to one side edge of the center block. Repeat around remaining edges of the center block.

6. Stitch the diagonal edge of a white on red E piece to the diagonal edge of a rose on white E piece to make a square. Make 32 squares in this way. *Note:* If desired, follow the instructions for right triangles, under Quick-and-Easy Methods on page 14, to make these squares.

7. Refer to Figure 3a to arrange the squares and pieces D and F. Join pieces in the sequence indicated to make 8 strips.

8. Refer to Figure 3b and make 8 strips as shown.

9. Refer to Figure 4. With right sides together, stitch the strips made in steps 7 and 8 to the edges of the C pieces as shown.

10. Refer to Figure 5. Join the muslin G and H pieces as shown.

To join borders

1. Join one short border strip to the top edge of the completed patchwork piece. Repeat on the bottom edge.

2. Join the remaining border strips to the side edges of the patchwork piece.

To quilt

1. Trace the quilting patterns on pattern pieces G and H and transfer to the pillow top (see page 11).

2. With batting between, pin the pillow top to one white square.

3. Using small running stitches, quilt along marked lines.

To finish

1. Pin the remaining white square (backing) to the pillow top.

2. Stitch around 4 corners and 3 sides, leaving one edge open for turning.

3. Trim the corners and the seam allowances.

4. Turn right side out and press. Turn the raw edges to the wrong side ¼ inch and press.

5. Insert pillow form or fill with stuffing and slipstitch the opening closed.

Figure 2

Figure 3a

Figure 3b

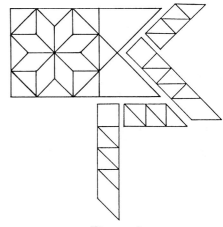

Figure 4

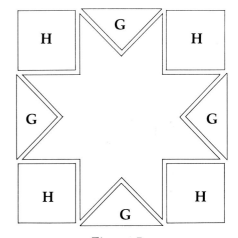

Figure 5

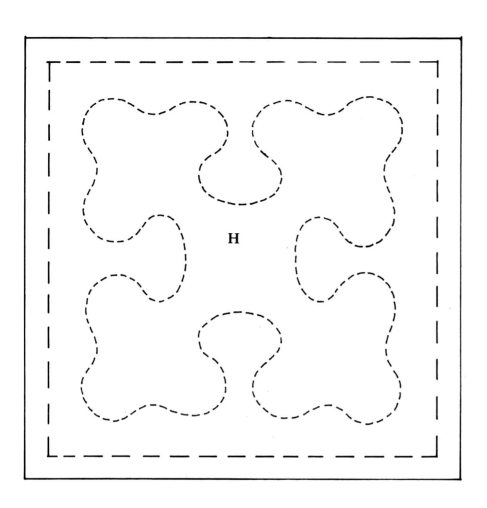

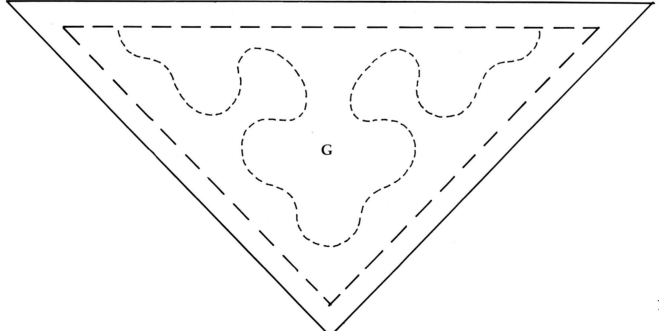

119

✦ DRESDEN PLATE ✦ OLD AND NEW

In our town there are auctions and yard sales every Saturday. Finding a bargain is the local passion. There are always several quilts, but they are usually quite expensive. Now and then, however, you can find one in terrible condition that's offered for practically nothing. Never pass up a worn, torn quilt; you'd be surprised at how many projects you can get out of the good parts of a badly worn quilt. Often rips and tears can be repaired.

Such was the case with a pretty Dresden Plate quilt that I found at a yard sale. The print fabrics are all from the 1920s and 30s. Some of the colors are pleasantly faded, but the sashing strips have retained their bright blue color. The background fabric was stained and there were spatters of paint here and there. Still, there were enough good blocks to make several pillows. I replaced about six patchwork pieces by carefully stitching the same size fabric over the ripped areas.

Not only did I get pillows from the quilt, but I was able to make a four-square table cover, and a two-square tote. The straps of the tote were made by piecing together some of the sashing strips. Admittedly, they are a bit frayed, but they're still acceptable. Finally, I cut away the entire Dresden Plate design from one square with a badly stained background and made this into an appliqué for the back of my jean jacket. It was fun to see how many projects I could get from this one single quilt.

To make these projects from scratch you'll need a variety of prints, plus a solid color for the borders. You may notice that my projects are a bit irregular in places. For example, checkerboard patchwork squares appear on some borders but not on others. This is because the good blocks were cut away from the quilt and stitched together differently. I've simplified the directions for making the following projects to reflect a more accurate and traditional technique, and have tried to improve on the design. Therefore, your finished project may not look exactly like the photograph (it may look even better)!

Pillow

Finished Size: 16 x 16 inches

Materials

Note: Yardages are figured for fabric 45 inches wide.

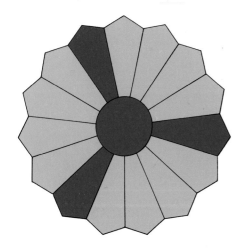

120

¼ yard blue fabric
½ yard muslin (includes backing)
a variety of print fabric scraps
tracing paper
thin cardboard
thin quilt batting, 16 x 16 inches
16-inch pillow form or polyester stuffing

Directions

Note: All measurements include ¼-inch seam allowance. Join all pieces with right sides together, taking ¼-inch seams. Press seams to one side.

    Trace pattern pieces A and B, transfer to thin cardboard and cut out to make templates (see page 11). To cut the fabric pieces using each template, place the template on the wrong side of the fabric indicated, trace around the outline and cut out, adding ¼-inch seam allowances all around.

Cut the following:

from blue:
    2 strips, each 2 x 13½ inches (for top and bottom borders)
    2 strips, each 2 x 16½ inches (for side borders)
    1 B
    3 A

from print fabric scraps:
    12 A

from muslin:
    1 square, 13½ x 13½ inches
    1 square, 16½ x 16½ inches (backing)

To make appliqué

1. Place the A template on the wrong side of each corresponding print fabric piece and press the seam allowance over the template on each side of the pointed end only.
2. Remove the template and press the fabric again to sharpen the crease.
3. Refer to Figures 1a-b. Join a blue A piece to a print A piece along one long edge as shown.
4. Next, join 3 more print A pieces in the same way.
5. Next, join a blue A piece, followed by 4 print A pieces, then a blue A piece and 4 more print A pieces.
6. Join the last print A piece to the raw edge of the first blue A piece to complete the circle.

Figure 1a

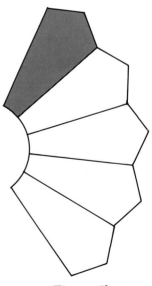

Figure 1b

To apply appliqué

1. Center and pin the smaller muslin square to the quilt batting.
2. Center the patchwork plate on the muslin square and pin in place.
3. Next, center the cardboard B template on the wrong side of the corresponding blue fabric circle and clip into the seam allowance all around.
4. Press the clipped seam allowance over the edge of the template.

5. Remove the template, press the edges again, and pin the fabric circle in the center of the Dresden Plate on the muslin, as shown in Figure 2.
6. Using a slipstitch through all 3 layers, sew the turned edges of the entire appliqué to the muslin and batting.

To join borders

1. Join the shorter blue border strips to the top and bottom edges of the pillow top.
2. Repeat with the remaining border strips on the side edges of the pillow top.

To quilt

Take small running stitches ¼ inch away from each side of all seamlines and edges of the appliqué and borders.

To finish

1. Pin the pillow top and muslin backing together.
2. Stitch around 3 sides and 4 corners, leaving one edge open for turning.
3. Trim corners and seam allowances and turn right side out. Press.
4. Insert pillow form or fill with stuffing.
5. Turn the raw edges to the wrong side ¼ inch and press.
6. Slipstitch the opening closed.

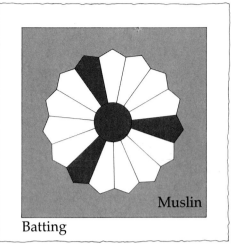

Figure 2

DRESDEN PLATE OLD AND NEW PATTERNS

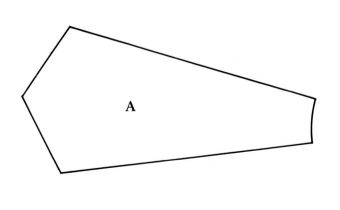

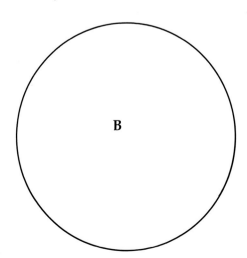

Holiday Table Cover

Finished Size: 33½ x 33½ inches

Materials

Note: Yardages are figured for fabric 45 inches wide.

½ yard blue fabric
2 yards muslin (includes backing)
a variety of print fabric scraps
tracing paper
thin cardboard
1 yard thin quilt batting

Directions

Note: All measurements include ¼-inch seam allowance. Join all pieces with right sides together, taking ¼-inch seams. Press seams to one side (the blue side, where applicable).

Trace pattern pieces A and B, transfer to thin cardboard and cut out to make templates (see page 11). To cut the fabric pieces using each template, place the template on the wrong side of the fabric indicated, trace around the outline and cut out, adding ¼-inch seam allowances all around.

Cut the following:

from blue:
   2 strips, each 2 x 31 inches (for top and bottom borders)
   2 strips, each 2 x 34 inches (for side borders)
   4 strips, each 2 x 15 inches, and
   4 strips, each 2 x 13½ inches, for sashing strips
   4 B
   12 A

from print scraps:
   48 A

from muslin:
   1 square, 34 x 34 inches (backing)
   2 strips, each 2 x 14½ inches
   1 strip, 2 x 31 inches
   4 squares, each 13½ x 13½ inches

To make appliqués

1. Follow Pillow directions under "To make appliqué," steps 1 through 6.
2. Make 4 in this way.

To apply appliqué

1. Follow Pillow directions under "To apply appliqué," steps 2 through 5.
2. Slipstitch the turned edges of each appliqué to the muslin.

To make unit 1

1. Refer to Figures 3a and 3b. Join a 2 x 13½-inch sashing strip to the right side edge of a patchwork square.

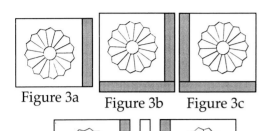

Figure 3a   Figure 3b   Figure 3c

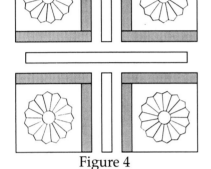

Figure 4

Figure 5

2. Join a 2 x 15-inch sashing strip to the bottom edge of the patchwork square.

3. Make 2 in this way.

To make unit 2

1. Refer to Figure 3c. Join a 2 x 13½-inch sashing strip to the left side edge of a patchwork square.

2. Join a 2 x 15-inch sashing strip to the bottom edge of the patchwork square.

3. Make 2 in this way.

To join squares

1. Refer to Figure 4. Arrange the squares as shown.

2. Join a 2 x 14½-inch muslin strip to the blue right-hand edge of one unit 1 patchwork square as shown.

3. Join a unit 2 patchwork square to the other long raw edge of the muslin strip as shown to make the top row.

4. Repeat with the remaining blocks to make the bottom row.

5. Join a 2 x 31-inch muslin strip to the bottom edge of the top row of squares.

6. Next, join the top edge of the bottom row of squares to the muslin strip.

To join borders

1. Refer to Figure 5. Join one 2 x 31-inch border strip to the top edge of the patchwork fabric.

2. Repeat on the bottom edge of the patchwork fabric.

3. Join the remaining border strips to the side edges of the patchwork top (Figure 6).

To quilt

1. With wrong sides together and batting between, pin patchwork top, batting and backing together.

2. Starting at the center and working outward in a sunburst pattern, take long, loose, basting stitches through all layers.

3. Take small running stitches ¼ inch away from each side of all seam-lines and edges of appliqué and borders. Do not quilt into the seam allowances around the outer edges.

To finish

1. When all quilting is complete, remove pins and basting stitches. Trim batting to ¼ inch smaller than top and backing all around.

2. Turn the raw edges of the top and backing fabric to the wrong side ¼ inch and press. Pin pressed edges together.

3. Machine-stitch or slipstitch all around.

Figure 6

126

Tote Bag

Finished Size: 16 x 16 inches

Materials

Note: Yardages are figured for fabric 45 inches wide.

½ yard blue fabric
½ yard fabric for lining (use same blue fabric,
    muslin, or fabric to match one of the scraps
    for the appliqué)
½ yard muslin
a variety of print fabric scraps
tracing paper
thin cardboard
½ yard thin quilt batting

Directions

Note: All measurements include ¼-inch seam allowance.

Trace pattern pieces A and B, transfer to thin cardboard and cut out to make templates (see page 11). To cut the fabric pieces, place the template on the wrong side of the fabric indicated, trace around the outline and cut out, adding ¼-inch seam allowances all around.

Cut the following:

from blue:
    4 strips, each 2 x 13½ inches (for top and bottom borders)
    4 strips, each 2 x 16½ inches (for side borders)
    2 strips, each 2 x 36 inches, for straps
    2 B
    6 A

from print fabric scraps:
    24 A

from muslin:
    2 squares, each 13½ x 13½ inches

from lining fabric:
    1 piece, 16½ x 32½ inches

from quilt batting:
    2 squares, each 16 x 16 inches

To make appliqué

Follow Pillow directions under "To apply appliqué," steps 1 through 6. Make 2 in this way.

To apply appliqué

1. Center and pin each patchwork plate on a muslin square.
2. Follow directions for Pillow under "To apply appliqué," steps 3 through 5.
3. Slipstitch the turned edges of each appliqué to the muslin.

To join borders

1. Join the shorter border strips to the top and bottom edges of the 2 patchwork squares.
2. Repeat with the remaining border strips on the side edges of each patchwork square.

To quilt

1. Pin each patchwork square to a square of quilt batting.
2. Take small running stitches through all 3 layers ¼ inch away from each side of all seamlines and edges of the appliqués and borders.

To make straps

1. Turn the long raw edges of 2 blue strips under ¼ inch and press.
2. Pin with wrong sides together and stitch along both long edges.
3. Repeat with the 2 remaining strips.

To make lining

1. With right sides together fold the lining fabric in half crosswise and press.
2. Stitch along the side edges. Trim seam allowances, but do not turn right side out.

To assemble bag

1. With right sides together, pin the appliquéd front and back together and stitch along both sides and the bottom edge, leaving the top edge open.
2. Trim seam allowances and corners and turn right side out. Press.
3. Slip the lining inside the bag and align the side seams of the lining to the side seams of the outer bag.
4. Turn the raw edges along the top to the wrong side ¼ inch and press.

5. Insert the short ends of the straps between the lining and the outer bag near the side seams and pin in position. The straps should meet at the seams. Try the bag over your shoulder or over your arm so you can adjust the length of the straps for your comfort. If they seem too long, cut off a little fabric from one end of each strap and reposition. Pin in place.

6. Machine-stitch all around the top edge of the bag, catching in the straps.

Jacket Appliqué

The Dresden Plate appliqué is fun to make and can be used to decorate a variety of clothing objects. I used it on my jean jacket, but it could be applied to the back of a sweatshirt, T-shirt, blouse, backpack or an existing tote bag.

Simply follow the directions for making the Dresden Plate appliqué as given for the Pillow project, and slipstitch it in place on your clothing. If you want to quilt the appliqué before applying it, pin the pieced plate to thin quilt batting and a backing fabric (such as muslin) cut to the shape of the appliqué. Take small running stitches ¼ inch away from each side of all inside seamlines. Then slipstitch the quilted appliqué in place all around.

♦ PATCHWORK ♦ STORAGE BOX

Nancy Moore padded the top of a plain pine box, then made a patchwork cover to fit. The top lifts up for easy access to storage, and the box itself can be used as an ottoman. If you turn to page 61 you can see how easily this project becomes a toy box with a different design. The box shown here is 14 x 17 inches, but the technique can be applied to any size item. For example, you might consider making a padded top for a jewelry box. For this project you will need a staple gun or upholstery tacks to attach the fabric to the box, and a decorative braid to cover the tacks, if used.

Finished Size: 14 x 17 inches or to fit your box

Materials

Note: Yardages are figured for fabric 45 inches wide.

⅛ yard brown calico
⅜ yard tan floral print fabric
1 yard bleached muslin
thick quilt batting or foam rubber for padding
tracing paper
cardboard
staple gun, or upholstery tacks, decorative
    braid and glue

Note: All measurements include ¼-inch seam allowance. Join all pieces with right sides together, taking ¼-inch seams. Press seams to one side.

Trace patterns A, B, C, D and E on page 135 and transfer to cardboard for templates (see page 11).

Cutting List

Cut the following:

from brown calico:
    4 C
    4 D

from tan floral print:
    2 strips, each 2½ x 12½ inches
    2 strips, each 2½ x 16½ inches
    4 A
    8 B
    1 E

from muslin:
    2 strips, each 6½ x 16½ inches
    2 strips, each 6½ x 28½ inches
    4 A
    16 B

Directions

To make block

1. Refer to Figure 1. Stitch the diagonal edge of a tan floral B piece to the diagonal edge of a muslin B piece to make a square as shown. Make 8 squares in this way.

2. Refer to Figure 2. Stitch the diagonal edge of a muslin B piece to each short edge of a brown calico C piece to make a rectangle. Make 4 rectangles in this way.

Figure 1   Figure 2

 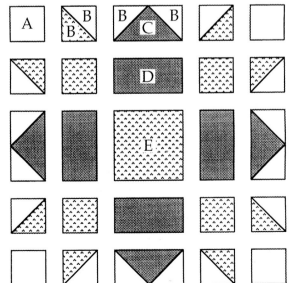

Figure 3a

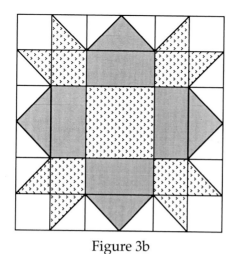

Figure 3b

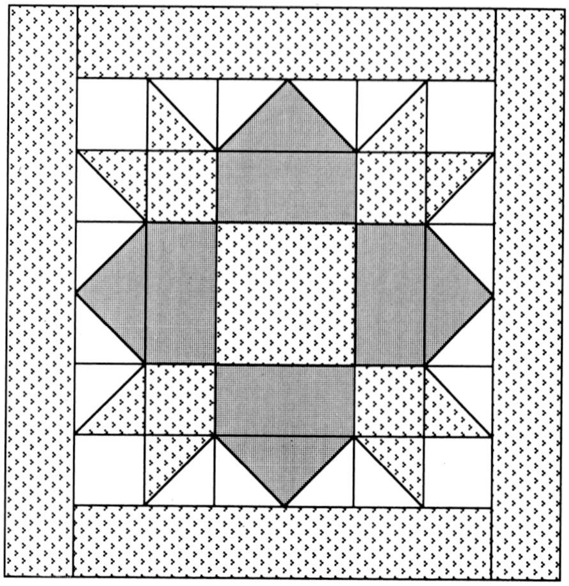

Figure 4

3. Refer to Figure 3a. Arrange the squares made in step 1, rectangles made in step 2, and all remaining A, D and E pieces as shown.
4. Join the pieces to form rows.
5. Join the bottom edge of the top row to the top edge of the second row.
6. Continue to join all 5 rows in this way to make the block shown in Figure 3b.

To join borders

1. Refer to Figure 4. Stitch one short tan floral strip to each side edge of the block.
2. Next, stitch the long tan floral strips to the top and bottom edges of the block.
3. Stitch one short muslin strip to each side edge of the block.
4. Next, stitch the remaining muslin strips to the top and bottom edges of the block.
Note: If you are making a top for a larger box, add more borders or make the muslin border strips wider and longer to obtain the needed size.

To finish

1. Cut quilt batting or foam rubber to fit the top of the box.
2. Center the patchwork fabric over the padding and pull the edges down taut over the sides. Use a staple gun to attach the fabric edges to the underside of the top of the box. Or you can turn the raw edges of the fabric under ¼ inch and attach it around the outside rim of the box top with small upholstery tacks. If you do, cover the tacks by gluing decorative braid all around to create a neat trim.

PATCHWORK STORAGE BOX PATTERNS

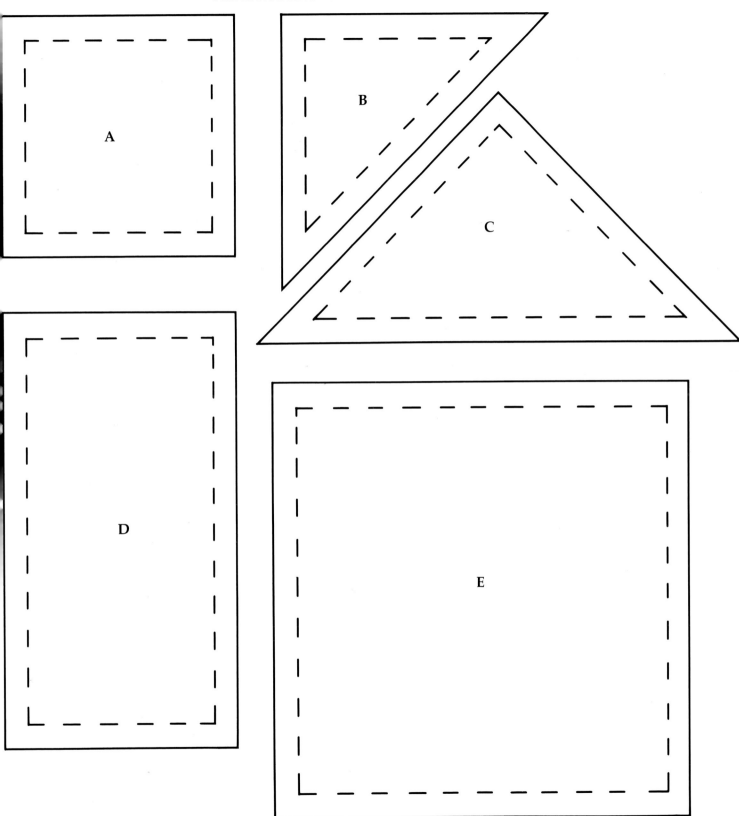

POTHOLDERS ✦ WITH PIZZAZZ

Potholders are ideal projects to make from fabric remnants. If your mother or grandmother has fabric scraps gathering dust in a sewing basket you may be able to create potholders reminiscent of an earlier time. My mother-in-law saves fabric and always seems to have just the right colors and patterns for all sorts of projects like these. The directions for making both potholders are exactly the same. The pattern is created with 1½-inch squares. However, they don't look identical because each is made with different fabric prints and colors. Materials and instructions for Potholder 1 (top) are given first, followed by changes for Potholder 2 (bottom) in parentheses.

Potholder 1 (2)

Finished Size: 9½ x 9½ inches

Materials
scraps of fabric in the following colors:
> green print, large floral print, small floral print, yellow print (red floral print, green floral print, pink floral print, purple floral print)

For each:
blue backing fabric, 11 x 11 inches
scraps of white fabric
quilt batting, 9½ x 9½ inches
plastic ring

Directions

Note: All measurements and templates include ¼-inch seam allowance. Join all pieces with right sides together, taking ¼-inch seams. Press seams to one side.

1. Trace pattern pieces A, B and C and transfer to heavy paper for templates (see page 11).
2. Use the templates to trace the outlines on the wrong side of the fabric as indicated in the following cutting directions.

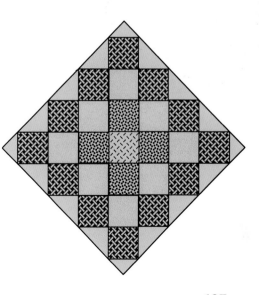

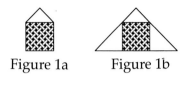

Figure 1a   Figure 1b

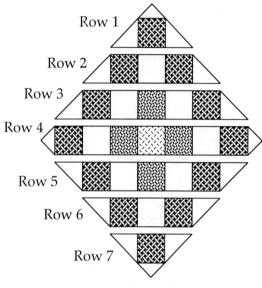

Figure 1c

Cut the following:

from green print (red floral print):
    12 A

from large print (green floral print):
    8 A

from small floral print (pink floral print):
    4 A

from yellow print (purple floral print):
    1 A

from white:
    12 B
    4 C

To make rows

1. Refer to color photograph and Figure 1a. Stitch a small white triangle to one side of a green (red) square as shown.
2. Refer to color photograph and Figure 1b. Stitch a large white triangle to each side edge of the green (red) square as shown. Make 2 for rows 1 and 7.
3. Refer to photograph and Figure 1c. Join a green (red) square to a large floral print (green floral print) square along one side edge.
4. Join another green (red) square to the opposite side of the large floral print (green floral print) square as shown.
5. Next, join a large white triangle to each side edge of this row of squares. Make 2 for rows 2 and 6.
6. Stitch a large white triangle to one side edge of a green (red) square followed by a large floral print (green floral print) square, then a small floral (pink floral) square, then another large floral print (green floral) square, then a green (red) square, and end with a large white triangle. Make 2 for rows 3 and 5.
7. For row 4, stitch a small white triangle to one side edge of a green (red) square. Join a large floral (green floral print) to the opposite side of the green (red) square, followed by a small floral print (pink floral) square, followed by a yellow (purple) square, then another small floral (pink floral) square, a large floral (green floral) square, another green (red) square, and end the row with a small white triangle as shown.

To join rows

1. Refer to Figure 1c. With seams aligned, join the bottom edge of row 1 to the top edge of row 2.
2. Continue to join rows as shown (Figure 2).

To quilt

1. Center the batting on the wrong side of the blue backing fabric. Place the patchwork piece right side up on top. There will be extra backing fabric all around.
2. Pin all 3 layers together.
3. Take small running stitches ¼ inch away from each side of all seamlines.

To finish

1. Turn the raw edges of the backing fabric under ¼ inch and press.
2. Bring the remaining backing fabric forward over the raw edges of the front of the potholder. Press and pin all around.
3. Machine-stitch or slipstitch in place.
4. Attach a plastic ring to the back of one corner for hanging.

POTHOLDERS WITH PIZZAZZ PATTERNS

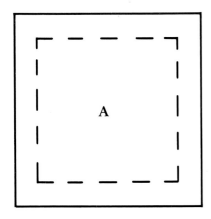

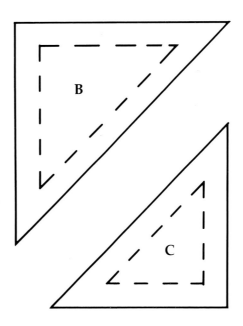

◆ TYLER'S FIRST ◆ QUILT

My husband, Douglas, and I just had our first baby. My mother-in-law, Nancy Moore, often works with me making quilts and other sewing projects, so of course Tyler's arrival was the perfect excuse to make a baby quilt. Since we are a boating family (Doug and I run a marine service on Cape Cod and his parents are in the custom sailmaking business), a nautical color scheme seemed appropriate. As you can see from the photograph, Tyler is quite cozy and comfortable sleeping soundly under his first quilt.

This is an easy pattern to make as a first project if you are a beginning quilter. The squares are tied rather than quilted, but you can add hand quilting if you're not in a rush to finish the quilt.

Finished Size: Approximately 34 x 42 inches

Materials

Note: Yardages are figured for fabric 45 inches wide.

1¼ yards blue calico
1¾ yards bleached muslin
quilt batting, 34 x 42 inches
1 skein blue embroidery floss
tracing paper
cardboard

Cutting List

Note: All measurements and patterns include ¼-inch seam allowance. Join all pieces with right sides together, taking ¼-inch seams. Press seams to the dark side.

Trace patterns A and B and transfer them to cardboard for templates (see page 11).

Cut the following:

from blue:
>   2 strips, each 3 x 35 inches (for side borders)
>   2 strips, each 4½ x 34¼ inches (for top and bottom borders)
>   15 A
>   60 B

from muslin:
    1 piece 34¼ x 43 inches (backing)
    15 A
    60 B

Directions

To make blocks

Block 1

Figure 1a

1. Refer to Figure 1a. Join the diagonal edge of a muslin B piece to each edge of a blue A piece to make a block.
2. Make 15 blocks in this way.

Block 2

Figure 1b

1. Refer to Figure 1b. Join the diagonal edge of a blue B piece to each edge of a muslin A piece to make a block.
2. Make 15 blocks in this way.

To make rows

1. Refer to Figure 2. With right sides together, join a block 1 to a block 2.
2. Continue with another block 1, then a block 2, and end with another block 1. Make 3 rows in this way for rows 1, 3 and 5.
3. Join a block 2 to a block 1.
4. Continue with a block 2, then another block 1, and end with a block 2. Make 3 rows in this way for rows 2, 4 and 6.

To join rows

Refer to Figure 3. Stitch the bottom edge of row 1 to the top edge of row 2. Continue to join all 6 rows in this way.

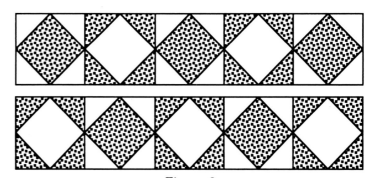

Figure 2

To join borders

1. Refer to Figure 3. Join a 3 x 34½-inch border strip to one side edge of the patchwork section. Repeat on the opposite side edge.
2. Join a 4½ x 35-inch border strip to the top edge, and the remaining strip to the bottom edge to complete the quilt top.

To tie-quilt

1. With wrong sides together and batting between, pin top, batting and backing fabric together.
2. Using 3 strands of embroidery floss, tie the quilt through all layers at the center of each block and at each corner of each block (see page 14).

To finish

1. Trim batting to ¼ inch smaller than the quilt top all around.
2. Trim backing to the same size as the quilt top.
3. Turn the raw edges of the backing and quilt top to the wrong side ¼ inch and press. Pin in place.
4. Machine-stitch or slipstitch the pressed edges all around.

Figure 3

TYLER'S FIRST QUILT PATTERNS

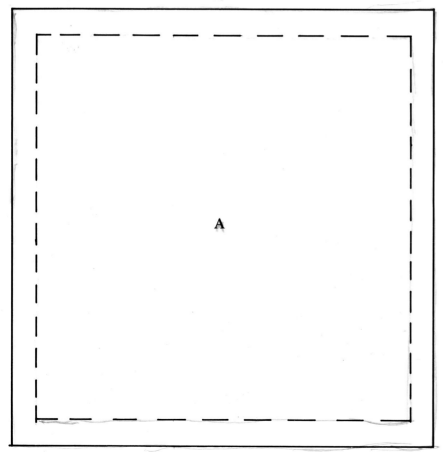

A

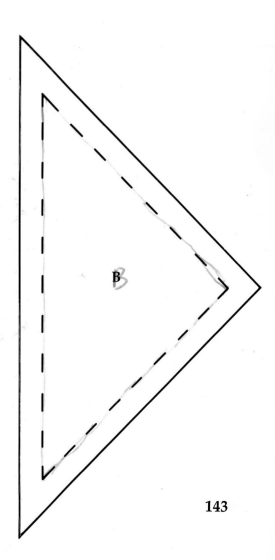

B

143

INDEX

All of us at Meredith® Press are dedicated to offering you, our customer, the best books we can create. We are particularly concerned that all of the instructions for making projects are clear and accurate. Please address your correspondence to: Customer Service Department, Meredith® Press, Meredith Corporation, 150 East 52nd Street, New York, NY 10022.

Nostalgia Patchwork & Quilting is the seventh in a series of quilting books. If you would like the first six books in the series, please write to: Better Homes and Gardens Books, P.O. Box 10670, Des Moines, IA 50309-3400, or call 1-800-678-2665.